UK LIGHT RAIL
and Tram Museum
GUIDE 2016

Written by James Millington

Edited by Nick Meskell

Design by Jason Prescott

Published by Train Crazy Publishing

© 2016 Train Crazy Publishing

Published by:
Train Crazy Publishing, Videoscene, PO Box 243, Lytham St Annes. FY8 9DE
email: sales@videoscene.co.uk

Contents

UK LIGHT RAIL
and Tram Museum
GUIDE 2016
Locations

Introduction

Welcome to our 2016 guide which is a fully rewritten and reworked edition. You'll notice straight away that we've changed the size of the guide this year. We accept that the text last year was probably too small and there were not enough photos. Working in the A6 format has its limitations, so here we are, bigger, brighter, glossier, more pages, more photos and all for the same price! We've included Docklands Light Railway and the Tyne and Wear Metro again. Although not trams as such, they still come under the light rail banner. The book is split into six chapters which feature 30 systems and/or museums and as a bonus this year - Cliff Lifts!

With ongoing extension work continuing in Manchester, Birmingham, Sheffield and Dublin and new lines opening in Nottingham, plus deliveries of further new trams, the second generation tram systems of Britain and Ireland are certainly flourishing right now. Passenger numbers continue to rise and although there are no completely new systems under construction at this time, almost all of the existing ones are planning extensions, and improvements.

I would like to thank all the contributors to this edition. The guide was written by James Millington. David Umpleby wrote the Docklands, Manx and Cliff Lift sections. I wrote the routes, services and timetable sections. A massive thank you is extended to everybody who provided images, especially Jason Cross and the individuals who contributed to the Cliff Lift section. Without your help this edition wouldn't have been possible.

Nick Meskell

Nick Meskell
March 2016

Content - The information provided in this book has been obtained from official sources as well as our observations when visiting the systems, updated to March 2016. The fleet lists provided are updated to 10th March 2016. The list of tram liveries is ever changing, particularly advertising liveries. These can last as little as a few weeks or be modified at short notice.

Maps - The maps used in this publication are our versions of the official maps published by the various operators. These are to be used only as a rough guide and connections to railway stations etc are not shown. Not all of the stops shown are open all of the day or at weekends and some do not have disabled or wheelchair access. Please use the official maps provided or check with the operator before travelling.

Front cover: Nottingham Express Transit Alstom Citadis 228 heads towards Clifton South on 3rd February 2016. *James Millington*

Back cover: Seaton 6 was built at Eastbourne in 1954 and is the oldest of the cars built by Modern Electric Tramways to remain on the tramway. Here it brings another full load back to the town during summer 2015. *James Millington*

Light Rail Metros

Docklands Light Railway
London

Vital Statistics

Opened: 1987

Operator: KeolisAmey Docklands Ltd

Number of lines: 4

Depots: Beckton and Poplar

Route mileage: 23 (37km)

Power supply: 750V DC third rail

Track gauge: 4ft 8 1/2in (1435mm)

Website: www.dlrlondon.co.uk

Background

Built between 1985 and 1987 at a cost of £77m, the DLR was formally opened on 30th July 1987 by Queen Elizabeth II. Normal services began on 31st August 1987.

The initial system had two routes - Tower Gateway to Island Gardens and Stratford to Island Gardens - with a total length of eight miles (13km) over 15 stations.

July 1991 saw the first major extension, which was a tunnel to the deep level tube station at Bank. Gaining access via a steep incline, the railway runs in twin tunnels. It allowed interchange with London Underground services on the Central, Circle, District, Northern and Waterloo & City lines, which saw an immediate huge increase in DLR patronage.

A major route extension opened in March 1994 from Poplar to Beckton via Canning Town,

The arrival platform at Bank is seen with unit 75 leading. 75 is one of 47 class B92s in service with DLR, built between 1993 and 1995. This platform is used for incoming trains which unload and run via a headshunt into the adjacent platform 9, the normal departure platform. This ensures a very fast turn around at Bank, making photography here a challenge! ***Jason Cross***

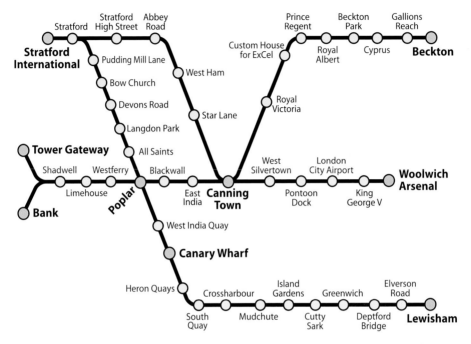

running along the north side of Royal Victoria Dock and Royal Albert Dock. Beckton depot opened in 1994, built on the site of the former Beckton gasworks.

In 2004 Mayor of London Ken Livingstone announced his five year investment plan for public transport. Part of this plan was a third extension to the DLR, possibly its most ambitious, which would see the DLR routed once again under the Thames, this time to Woolwich Arsenal.

2006 saw improvements to Beckton depot with expansion to 17 roads for storage, two carriage wash plants and a new state of the art control room. The first part of the new route to be opened was the easier part on raised sections to King George V dock in December 2005. This was followed by opening to Woolwich Arsenal some four years later on 12th January 2009.

The latest extension came in August 2011 as part of the transport upgrades provided for the 2012 Olympic Games. A line was built between the existing stations at Canning Town and Stratford, including four new stations, running on the former North London Line. A short extension was added from Stratford to Stratford International.

Routes and Services

Although not colour coded or numbered, the DLR has five principal operating routes: Bank to Woolwich Arsenal, Bank to Lewisham, Tower Gateway to Beckton, Stratford to Canary Wharf and Stratford International to Woolwich Arsenal. Of all the systems described in this book, the DLR operates the most intensive services with frequencies of up to every four minutes peak, five minutes off peak. A Saturday service operates on Good Friday. A Sunday service operates on all Bank Holidays.

Timetables

Bank to Woolwich Arsenal: From Bank the first trains are: 05.33 (M-S), 07.03 (Sun). Last trains are 00.33 (M-S) and 23.33 (Sun). From Woolwich Arsenal the first trains are: 05.28 (M-F), 05.31 (Sat), 07.01 (Sun). Last trains are: 00.24 (M-F), 00.11 (Sat), 23.11 (Sun). Trains run every ten minutes daily, increased to every eight minutes at peak times on weekdays.

Bank to Lewisham: From Bank the first trains are: 05.30 (M-S), 07.00 (Sun). Last trains are 00.30 (M-S) and 23.30 (Sun). From Lewisham the first trains are: 05.28 (M-S), 06.58 (Sun). Last trains are: 00.18 (M-S), 23.18 (Sun). On weekdays, trains run every five minutes, increased to every four minutes at peak times. At weekends early and late trains run at ten minute intervals, increasing to every five minutes for the majority of the day.

Tower Gateway to Beckton: From Tower Gateway the first trains are: 05.28 (M-S), 06.58 (Sun). Last trains are 23.48 (M-F), 23.49 (Sat) and 22.49 (Sun). From Beckton the first trains are: 05.29 (M-S), 06.59 (Sun). Last trains are: 00.29 (M-S), 23.29 (Sun). On weekdays trains run every ten minutes, increased to every eight minutes at peak times. At weekends trains are every ten minutes for most of the day.

Stratford International to Woolwich Arsenal: From Stratford International the first trains are: 05.30 (M-S), 07.00 (Sun). Last trains are 00.12 (M-S) and 23.12 (Sun). From Woolwich Arsenal the first trains are: 05.27 (M-S), 06.59 (Sun). Last trains are: 00.07 (M-S), 23.07 (Sun). On weekdays trains run every ten minutes, increased to every eight minutes at peak times. At weekends trains are every ten minutes for most of the day.

Stratford to Canary Wharf: From Stratford the first trains are: 05.28 (M-S), 06.58 (Sun). Last trains are 00.14 (M-S) and 23.14 (Sun). From Canary Wharf the first trains are: 05.29 (M-S), 06.59 (Sun). Last trains are: 00.39 (M-F), 00.30 (Sat), 23.30 (Sun). On weekdays trains run every five minutes, increased to every four minutes at peak times. At weekends trains are every five minutes for most of the day, with early and late trains at ten minute intervals.

Fares and Tickets

Docklands Light Railway falls within Transport for London's zonal fare system, with a zone 1 - 4 card needed. The DLR stations are mainly located in Zone 2 - 3, except for Bank and Tower Gateway (Zone 1) and Woolwich Arsenal (Zone 4).

A One Day Travelcard Anytime costs £12.10. Single cash fares are available from London Underground stations and London City Airport. Prices start at £4.90 (£4.20 on Oyster) for a Zone 1 adult single, and £5.90 (£3.90 peak on Oyster and £2.80 off peak) for a Zone 1 - 4 adult single. With a pre-loaded TfL Oystercard, Oyster's daily price cap at £9.30 offers the best value. The peak hours are Monday to Friday 06.30 to 09.30 and 16.00 to 19.00, all other times are off peak. Saturday and Sunday are off peak all day.

Beckton Depot with two class B07 type trams, easily discernable by their more modern black fronts. Beckton is the largest depot on the system and where the majority of the fleet are stabled and maintained. **David Umpleby**

Key Location

As the DLR has expanded, so has the number of key locations through which several routes pass and where you are guaranteed a regular passage of trains. However, despite the huge expansion of the system, Poplar depot, the original focal point of the network, has remained the central hotspot through which the majority of services pass. There are constant moves on and off the depot, especially around peak times, with Poplar offering close proximity to central London.

The DLR is closely linked in with other forms of public transport in the East End of London with connections to London Underground, the bus network and Emirates Airline! 103 - a B07 - is seen leading a three-car train from Stratford towards Stratford High Street, whilst a Jubilee Line Train made up of 1996 stock is led by 96018. The difference in size between the two types of rolling stock is very evident here. **Jason Cross**

The Fleet

Although several different classes of trains have been used on the DLR since it opened they have all been very similar in design, with the same basic principle. They are formed of articulated two car trains, each of which is referred to as one train and which carry the same fleet number. These pairs can be coupled to other pairs to make a longer set. For many years the maximum which could operate together was two sets, although further upgrade work on station platforms has seen this increased to three set operation.

The oldest vehicles in operation today are the B90 class, built in 1991-1992 by BN Construction in Belgium (now part of Bombardier), totalling 23. Following the success of the B90 class, a further 47 trains were ordered from BN Construction and designated as B92, built between 1993 and 1995.

Into the new millennium and additional stock was clearly needed. The new vehicles were designated as B2K and were built in 2002 and 2003, again by BN Construction in Belgium.

A change to the trend was the introduction of the B07 stock. Ordered in 2007, 55 units were built by Bombardier in Germany between 2007 and 2010. The units first entered service in 2008 and were the first on the DLR to operate as a three car train. Of note, the B07 stock can only work in multiple with others of the same type, whilst the B90, B92 and B2K stock are all compatible with each other.

The livery carried is uniform across the fleet and is an all over red with a blue curving stripe to denote the River Thames.

The Future

Several extensions have been investigated, most notably to Dagenham Dock, although there are no signs of this progressing at the moment.

When Crossrail opens fully in 2018, it will reduce the patronage of the DLR and relieve the pressure somewhat.

Fleet details:
23 B90, 2-section 6-axle cars built 1991-1992 by BN Construction, Belgium (Bombardier Transportation)
Motors: 2 x 140kw   **Seats:** 52+4

No.	Notes	No.	Notes
22		34	
23		35	
24		36	
25		37	
26		38	
27		39	
28		40	
29		41	
30		42	
31		43	
32		44	
33			

Fleet details:
47 B92, 2-section 6-axle cars built 1993-1995 by BN Construction, Belgium (Bombardier Transportation)
Motors: 2 x 140kw   **Seats:** 52+4

No.	Notes	No.	Notes
45		69	
46		70	
47		71	
48		72	
49		73	
50		74	
51		75	
52		76	
53		77	
54		78	
55		79	
56		80	
57		81	
58		82	
59		83	
60		84	
61		85	
62		86	
63		87	
64		88	
65		89	
66		90	
67		91	
68			

Fleet details:
24 B2K, 2-section 6-axle cars built 1993-1995 by BN Construction, Belgium (Bombardier Transportation)
Motors: 2 x 140kw   **Seats:** 52+4

No.	Notes	No.	Notes
92		05	
93		06	
94		07	
95		08	
96		09	
97		10	
98		11	
99		12	
01		13	
02		14	
03		15	
04		16	

Fleet details:
55 B07, 2-section 6-axle cars built 2007-2010 by Bombardier, Germany
Motors: 2 x 140kw   **Seats:** 52+4

No.	Notes	No.	Notes
101		129	
102		130	
103		131	
104		132	
105		133	
106		134	
107		135	
108		136	
109		137	
110		138	
111		139	
112		140	
113		141	
114		142	
115		143	
116		144	
117		145	
118		146	
119		147	
120		148	
121		149	
122		150	
123		151	
124		152	
125		153	
126		154	
127		155	
128			

Tyne and Wear Metro

Vital Statistics

Opened: 1980
Operator: Nexus
Number of lines: Two
Depot: Gosforth
Route mileage: 46.3 (74.5km)
Power supply: 1500V DC overhead line
Track gauge: 4ft 8½in (1435mm)
Website: www.nexus.org.uk/metro

Background

The Tyne and Wear Metro is a rapid transit suburban rail network serving the North East areas of Newcastle upon Tyne, Gateshead, North and South Tyneside and Sunderland. The system opened in stages between 1980 and 1984 and was the second modernised suburban railway in the UK following on from the Merseyrail network. It is credited as the first modern light rail network in the UK, albeit with no street running.

Two extensions have been built over the succeeding years: Bank Foot to Newcastle Airport opened in 1991 and from Pelaw to South Hylton, Sunderland, in 2002. The Sunderland extension took Metrocars onto Network Rail tracks between Pelaw and Sunderland, pioneering the principle of shared track operation between light and heavy rail in the UK.

4056 leads a two car train to Monkseaton, seen at Benton on 2nd October 2015. **Jason Cross**

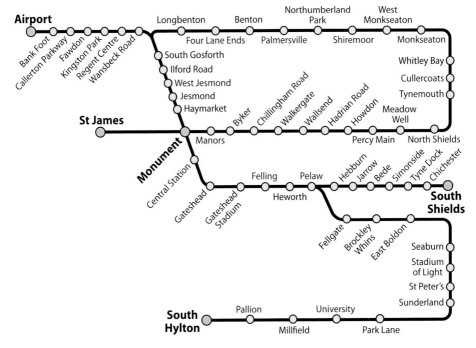

Routes and Services

Two basic services are in operation:

Green Line: Airport – Monument - South Hylton

Yellow Line: St. James – Monument – North Shields – Monument - South Shields

Timetable

Green Line: From Airport the first trains are: 05.37 (M-F), 05.42 (Sat), 06.29 (Sun) and the last trains are 23.59 (daily). From South Hylton the first trains are: 06.04 (M-F), 06.05 (Sat), 07.06 (Sun) and the last trains are 23.47 (daily). Mondays to Saturdays, the daytime off peak service is every 12 minutes, then every 15 minutes in the evening. Additional trains run at peak times. On Sundays, trains are every 15 minutes for most of the day.

Yellow Line: From St. James the first trains are: 06.02 (M-F), 06.17 (Sat), 07.02 (Sun) and the last trains are 23.38 (daily). From South Shields the first trains are: 05.45 (M-F), 05.51 (Sat), 07.03 (Sun) and the last trains are 23.56 (daily). Mondays to Saturdays, the daytime off peak service is every 12 minutes, then every 15 minutes in the evening. Additional trains run at peak times. On Sundays, trains are every 15 minutes for most of the day. Note: Empty stock workings are not detailed, but all trains start and finish each day at Gosforth depot.

Tyne and Wear Metro

4026 is seen leading a two train set at Felling on a South Shields to St James service on 25th July 2014. Both the sets are seen in the earlier Tyne & Wear livery. This version of the livery makes the 'Metrocars' look considerably older than the black and yellow livery which is now being rolled out across the fleet. Compared to most other light rail systems the Tyne and Wear, in common with the area in general is grossly under funded, hence the use of trains that are now over 30 years old. *Jason Cross*

Fares and Tickets

At-station ticket machines on all platforms: Single, daily and weekly tickets available, with the Day Saver all zones ticket at £4.80 offering good value for exploring the system (it is also valid on the Shields Ferry). There is no child equivalent; children under 16 can purchase a one day Junior Rover at £3.90, which includes unlimited travel on all modes across Tyne and Wear. Families should buy a North East Explorer Ticket at £19.50.

Key Location

The section of the system from South Gosforth to Pelaw is shared by both Green Line and Yellow Line services, with trains operating at up to every six minutes along this section. South Gosforth station features an attractive North Eastern Railway footbridge between the two platforms, making this a particularly attractive spot for photographs.

The Fleet

The fleet consists of 90 high floor light rail 'Metrocars', supplied by Metro Cammell, Birmingham. Prototype units 4001 and 4002 were constructed in 1975 for testing on the Metro test track, and were followed by production examples 4003 to 4090 between 1978 and 1981. They are single articulated, bi-directional vehicles mounted on three bogies, of which the outer two are powered. Each vehicle originally seated 68, and can accommodate 232 standing passengers. All 90 units were delivered in the cadmium yellow and white livery then carried by buses of the Tyne & Wear PTE, this livery lasting on the Metrocars until the mid-1990s. The replacement scheme featured a random application of green, red or blue, with yellow triangles on the doors and a yellow 'wedge' at each end. Following the development of shared

4004 leaves Jesmond on a service to Airport on 25th July 2014. **Jason Cross**

running with Network Rail on the Sunderland line from 2002, they are categorised as class 994 under the British Rail (BR) TOPS numbering system.

Between 2010 and 2015, 86 of the 90 units were refurbished by Wabtec at Doncaster. Work included corrosion treatment, new flooring and seating, and the installation of a larger wheelchair bay. This reduced the seating capacity to 64 and is set to extend the life of the present fleet to 2025. On completion the units received a new black livery with yellow doors and end warning panel. Due to budget constraints, four remain unrefurbished: prototype sets 4001 and 4002, plus 4040 and 4083 of the production fleet. These four are now electrically incompatible with the remainder of the fleet and will be held in reserve for use at times of exceptional demand. Of note, 4001 carries the original 1975 livery style, but with all-yellow doors to conform to rail vehicle accessibility regulations.

A very clean and smart looking 4069 is seen departing Callerton Parkway with a service to South Hylton from Airport on 24th July 2014. The true railway feel to the line is obvious here. **Jason Cross**

The Future

Various proposals for extensions have been submitted, including on-street tram lines to expand the network to regions with no current rail access. Funding options for appear to be limited, however.

A three-phase programme of upgrading the Tyne & Wear Metro with refurbished vehicles, stations and improved facilities has been completed up to Phase 2. Phase 3, to include the re-equipping of the system with new signalling and brand new vehicles, is expected to commence in 2019, although no funding has yet been secured for this final phase.

Tyne and Wear have several locomotives which are used on all forms of engineering trains. Two locomotives were due to be top and tailed on this leaf buster train, however with only one locomotive available a passenger train had to be used on the other end, in this case 4042, making a very strange sight! The locomotive is a Hunslet product. Working from Chillingham Road to Gosforth Depot on 2nd October 2015. **Jason Cross**

70

Fleet details:
90 2-section 6-axle cars built 1975, 1978-1981 by Metro Cammell, Birmingham
Seating: 64 (68 on unrefurbished examples) and 232 standing
Equipment: 2 x 187kw

No.	Notes	No.	Notes
4001	unrefurbished	4046	
4002	unrefurbished	4047	
4003		4048	
4004		4049	
4005		4050	
4006		4051	
4007		4052	
4008		4053	
4009		4054	
4010		4055	
4011		4056	
4012		4057	
4013		4058	
4014		4059	
4015		4060	
4016		4061	
4017		4062	
4018		4063	
4019		4064	
4020		4065	
4021		4066	
4022		4067	
4023		4068	
4024		4069	
4025		4070	
4026		4071	
4027		4072	
4028		4073	
4029		4074	
4030		4075	
4031		4076	
4032		4077	
4033		4078	
4034		4079	
4035		4080	
4036		4081	
4037		4082	
4038		4083	unrefurbished
4039		4084	
4040	unrefurbished	4085	
4041		4086	
4042		4087	
4043		4088	
4044		4089	
4045		4090	

Modern Tramways

Manchester Metrolink

Vital Statistics

Opened: 1992
Operator: RAPT Group
Number of lines: Six
Depots: Trafford and Queen's Road
Route mileage: 58 (93 km)
Power supply: 750V DC overhead line
Track gauge: 4ft 8½in (1435mm)
Website: www.metrolink.co.uk

Background

Manchester Metrolink was inaugurated in 1992 as the first second generation tramway system in the UK. The original route from Bury in the north to Altrincham in the south reused former heavy rail lines connected across Manchester city centre with a brand new on-street alignment featuring a spur to Piccadilly Station. The original system achieved the long held ambition of linking Manchester's two principal railway stations, Piccadilly and Victoria.

Metrolink extended to Eccles in 1999/2000, but thereafter followed a decade of stagnation until 2010, when a spur to Media City was added onto the Eccles route.   This was to be the precursor of a massive expansion which saw routes added in stages from Trafford Bar on the Altrincham line to St. Werburgh's Road and East Didsbury in 2013, from Piccadilly Station to Droylsden and Ashton-under-Lyne between 2011 and 2013, and from Victoria to Oldham, Shaw and Crompton and Rochdale between 2012 and 2014.

Further expansion followed, with a diversion through Oldham town centre and an extension from St. Werburgh's Road to Manchester Airport, which both opened in 2014, bringing the network mileage to 57.5 miles.

The expanded system has put huge pressure on the original city centre routing, which is handling many more trams per hour than it was designed for. Plans for a second city crossing (2CC) were approved in October 2013 and completion of the initial section between Victoria and Exchange Square was achieved in December 2015. Preparation for 2CC has involved a substantial expansion of facilities at Deansgate-Castlefield, Victoria and at St. Peter's Square, where only a single track will be available throughout most of 2016 while the southern junction for 2CC is installed. The full 2CC is expected in 2017.

*A double set headed by 3040 departs Rochdale town centre for East Didsbury on 15th April 2015. **James Millington***

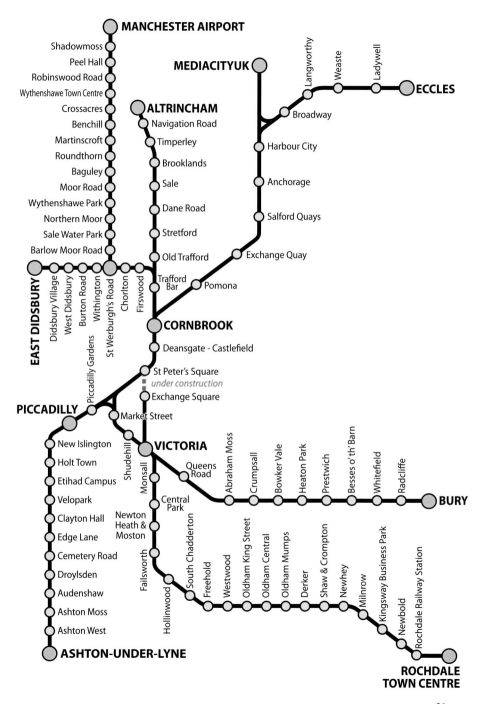

*Within the confines of Piccadilly Undercroft, 3077 trails a two car set about to take up a service to Eccles via MediaCityUK on 31st January 2015. **James Millington***

Routes and Services

As of spring 2016 there are six basic services in operation, plus two peak hour Monday to Saturday workings on both the Bury and Altrincham lines (which stay clear of St Peter's Square because of the current single track layout through this location due to engineering works in advance of 2CC) and slight Sunday variations.

A. Altrincham – Piccadilly – Etihad Campus

B. Altrincham – Deansgate-Castlefield (Monday to Saturday only)

C. Bury – Market Street – Victoria – East Didsbury

D. Bury – Victoria - Piccadilly (Monday to Saturday only)

E. Eccles – MediaCityUK – Piccadilly

F. Manchester Airport - Cornbrook

G. Rochdale – Oldham – Victoria - Piccadilly - Ashton-under-Lyne

H. Shaw and Crompton – Oldham – Victoria - Exchange Square

I. Rochdale – Oldham – Victoria – Exchange Square (Sunday only)

J. Ashton-under-Lyne – Droylsden – Piccadilly – Victoria (Sunday only)

All services operate on a 12 minute frequency. Services B and D run only between 07.30 and 20.00, and combine to provide a six minute frequency on both the Bury and Altrincham lines. Routes A, C and E are diagrammed to operate with double sets. This also helps to increase capacity through the city during the current operational restrictions through St. Peter's Square.

Timetable

Such is the scope of the Manchester system, it's not possible to list individual route timetables in detail and it is further complicated as they are split into four periods of operation: Mondays to Thursdays, Fridays, Saturdays and Sundays/Bank Holidays. Briefly, as an example, the first tram from Altrincham is 05.56 Mon to Sat, 06.48 Sun. Last tram is 23.44 Mon to Thu, 00.44 Fri and Sat and 22.47 Sun. From Manchester Airport, the first tram is 05.49 Mon to Sat, 06.48 Sun. Last tram is 23.25 Mon to Thu, 00.25 Fri and Sat and 22.32 Sundays. Unlike other systems which usually match Sunday evening timetables with weekday evenings, Metrolink services finish substantially earlier on Sundays, more than two hours earlier in some cases, compared to a Friday or Saturday. The Metrolink website provides an excellent summary of all routes:

www.metrolink.co.uk/tramtimes/Pages/default.aspx

Fares and Tickets

At-stop ticket machines on all platforms: Single, daily, weekly and period tickets available, with the off peak Day Travelcard at £5.00 (adult), £2.00 (child) and £6.20 (family) offering the best value for exploring the system.

Key Location

As Metrolink has expanded, so has the number of key locations through which several routes pass, and where you are always guaranteed a regular passage of trams. However the original focal point of the network, Piccadilly Gardens, has remained the central hotspot through which the majority of services pass on its triangular junction. With the onset of 2CC from 2017, Piccadilly Gardens will lose some significance as services will be divided between the original city centre routing and 2CC.

3029 leads a two car set into the Manchester bound platform at Oldham Mumps on 15th April 2015. **James Millington**

The Fleet

The operational fleet is made up exclusively of Bombardier M5000 Flexity Swift trams, built at Bautzen in Germany and delivered in stages since 2009. Initially ordered in low volumes to supplement the original Metrolink fleet and cater for capacity increases and route extensions, the decision to standardise on the type and abolish the old trams resulted in much larger orders in 2011/12, while further orders up to 2014 took the eventual total number of M5000s to 120, making it by far the largest class of tram in the UK. Completion of deliveries is expected during 2016. Fleet numbers are 3001 - 3120.

The M5000 vehicles are single articulated, bi-directional trams mounted on three bogies. Each tram seats 52 (with eight additional perch seats in wheelchair bays and the centre articulation), and can accommodate 146 standing passengers. All trams are to a high floor specification (Metrolink is a high floor system with full height platforms at all stops), and have been delivered

In the heart of Manchester city centre, 3056 heads through Piccadilly Gardens on its way to Rochdale on 31st May 2015.
James Millington

in the standard Metrolink livery of silver and yellow. From 3075 upwards, seating capacity is 60 with the perch seats reduced to six. The M5000s can operate singly or in coupled pairs.

Metrolink's original fleet consisted of 26 Italian built Ansaldo Firema T68 type light rail vehicles numbered 1001 – 1026 and delivered for the opening of the Phase 1 network in 1992. These were supplemented by six similar T68a trams supplied for the Eccles extension in 1999, and numbered 2001 – 2006.

Following the increase of the order for M5000 vehicles to include replacements for the T68 and T68a fleet, withdrawals commenced in April 2012 and were completed by January 2014. Most subsequently passed to Booths of Rotherham for disposal, although 1003 was acquired by the Greater Manchester Fire Service for training purposes, and four (1016, 1022, 1024 and 1026) have moved to Long Marston in Warwickshire for storage as part of the fleet of the UK Tram Consortium. 1007, 1020, 1023 and 2001 remain in store with Metrolink, with the former reserved for preservation by the Manchester Transport Museum Society.

The Future

Funding for an extension of Metrolink to the Trafford Centre (from Pomona on the Eccles line) was secured from the UK Treasury in November 2014, with completion of this line expected by 2020, and it remains the desire of Transport for Greater Manchester to construct a loop around Wythenshawe on the Airport line. Furthermore, it remains an aspiration of Rochdale Metropolitan Borough Council to see Metrolink extended to Middleton, and Tameside Metropolitan Borough Council would like to see the network extended to Stalybridge (from Ashton-under-Lyne). Transport for Greater Manchester is also keen to take Metrolink to Stockport from East Didsbury.

Tram-train proposals costed by Metrolink and TfGM could also see the network extended to Hale, Marple, Hadfield and Glossop, Hazel Grove, and Wigan.

1007 is one of just four of the older T68 and T68a trams remaining in stock with Metrolink, and is seen here at Altrincham during the T68 Farewell Tour on 26th May 2014. Reserved for preservation at Heaton Park, it is stored at Trafford Depot. **James Millington**

Manchester Metrolink

Operational fleet:
120 M5000 2-section 6-axle trams built 2008-2016 by Bombardier, Germany
Seating: 3001 – 3074: 52 (plus 8) and 146 standing. 3075 – 3120: 60 (plus 6) and 146 standing.
Equipment: Vossloh Kiepe/4 x 120kw Bombardier three-phase AC motors

No.	Name / Notes	No.	Name / Notes
3001		3042	
3002		3043	
3003		3044	
3004		3045	
3005		3046	
3006		3047	
3007		3048	
3008		3049	
3009	Coronation Street 50th Anniversary 1960-2010	3050	
3010		3051	
3011		3052	
3012		3053	
3013		3054	
3014		3055	
3015		3056	
3016		3057	
3017		3058	
3018		3059	
3019		3060	
3020	Lancashire Fusilier	3061	
3021		3062	
3022		3063	
3023		3064	
3024		3065	
3025		3066	
3026		3067	
3027		3068	
3028		3069	
3029		3070	
3030		3071	
3031		3072	
3032		3073	
3033		3074	
3034		3075	
3035		3076	
3036		3077	
3037		3078	
3038		3079	
3039		3080	
3040		3081	
3041		3082	

...continued

No.	Name / Notes	No.	Name / Notes
3083		3102	
3084		3103	
3085		3104	
3086		3105	
3087		3106	
3088		3107	
3089		3108	
3090		3109	
3091		3110	
3092		3111	
3093		3112	
3094		3113	
3095		3114	
3096		3115	
3097		3116	
3098		3117	
3099		3118	
3100		3119	
3101		3120	

Stored fleet:
3 T68 2-section 6-axle trams built 1991-1992 by Firema, Italy
Seating: 82 (plus 4) and 122 standing
Equipment: 4 x 105kw Ansaldo DC motors

No.	Withdrawn	Notes
1007	February 2014	Stored - Reserved for Manchester Transport Museum Society
1020	November 2012	Stored - Trafford depot
1023	January 2014	Stored - Trafford depot

Stored fleet:
1 T68a 2-section 6-axle cars built 1999 by Ansaldo, Italy
Seating: 82 (plus 4) and 122 standing
Equipment: 4 x 120kw Ansaldo three-phase AC motors

No.	Withdrawn	Notes
2001	April 2014	Stored - Trafford depot

Works vehicle:
Special Purpose Vehicle. 4-axle vehicle built 1991 by RFS Industries, South Yorkshire
Engine: Caterpillar

No.	Notes
1027	

Stagecoach Supertram
Sheffield

Vital Statistics

Opened: 1994
Operator: Stagecoach
Number of lines: Three
Depots: Nunnery
Route mileage: 18 (29km)
Power supply: 750V DC overhead line
Track gauge: 4ft 8½in (1435mm)
Website: www.supertram.net

Background

Sheffield's Supertram network opened in stages between 1994 and 1995 as the second of the UK's new generation of tramway systems. Originally operated by South Yorkshire Supertram Ltd (SYSL), a wholly owned subsidiary of South Yorkshire Passenger Transport Executive (SYPTE), SYSL was sold to the Stagecoach Group in 1997. Since this time, Stagecoach has been responsible for the operation of the system and the maintenance of the vehicles, although ownership of the trams and infrastructure remains with SYPTE.

Despite a number of proposed extensions, the size of the Supertram network has, until now, remained constant throughout its history. At the time of writing the network is still served exclusively by its original fleet of 25 Siemens/Duewag trams. However, following a number of Government led proposals for the introduction of tram-train technology to the UK, the Supertram network was selected for expansion to Rotherham using a freight only section of heavy rail route from Tinsley to Rotherham Parkgate. This will connect to the Supertram system via a newly constructed chord close to the existing Meadowhall South/Tinsley tram stop. Through services to Rotherham, using Supertram tracks as far as Cathedral, are expected to commence in 2017.

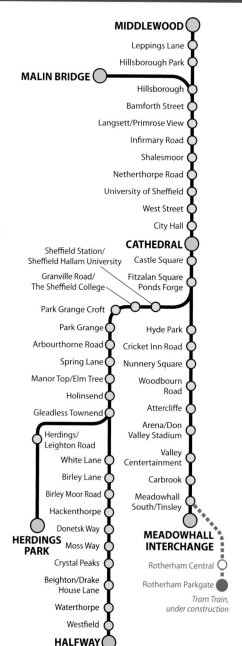

Routes and Services

The current system consists of three main arteries which link at a triangular junction at Park Square. As of spring 2016, three services are in operation:

Yellow: Meadowhall to Middlewood

Blue: Malin Bridge to Halfway

Purple: Cathedral to Herdings Park (extended from Cathedral to Meadowhall off-peak)

Tram services are supplemented by bus operated feeders SL1, SL2 and SL3, branded 'Supertramlink' and using buses in the distinctive tram livery. These connect with the Supertram network and provide services between Middlewood and Stocksbridge, Malin Bridge and Stannington, and Moss Way and Killamarsh via Crystal Peaks.

Timetable

Yellow route: The first tram from Meadowhall is 05.50 (M-F), 05.48 (Sat), 07.48 (Sun). The last tram is 00.03 (M-S), 23.43 (Sun). The first tram from Middlewood is 05.50 (M-F), 06.06 (Sat), 07.46 (Sun). The last tram is 00.04 (Mon-Sat), 23.44 (Sun). The yellow route service summary is every 10 minutes Mon-Sat peak, every 20 minutes Mon-Sat off peak and all day Sundays.

Blue route: The first tram from Malin Bridge is 05.56 (M-F), 05.59 (Sat), 07.59 (Sun). The last tram is 23.52 (M-S), 23.31 (Sun). The first tram from Halfway is 05.57 (M-F), 05.59 (Sat), 07.59 (Sun). The last tram is 00.10 (M-S), 23.51 (Sun). The blue route service summary is every 10 minutes Mon-Sat peak, every 20 minutes Mon-Sat off peak and all day Sundays.

Purple route: The first tram from Herdings Park is 05.55 (M-F), 05.57 (Sat), 08.02 (Sun). The last tram is 00.01 (M-S), 23.49 (Sun). The first tram from Cathedral is 06.21 (M-F), 06.22 (Sat), 07.39

East Midlands Trains advert liveried 116 arrives at Meadowhall with a yellow route service on 25th October 2015.
James Millington

(Sun). The last tram is 23.26 (M-F), 23.29 (Sat), 23.26 (Sun). The service summary is every 30 minutes Mon-Sat peak, every 20 minutes Mon-Sat off peak and all day Sundays. (This information comes from the official website. It is not known if the 30 minute peak frequency is an error as services are normally more frequent at peak times). Note: Empty stock workings are not detailed, but all trams start and finish each day at Nunnery depot.

117 calls at Sheffield Station on 28th March 2015 with a purple route service to Cathedral. **James Millington**

Fares and Tickets

Payable to conductor: Single, daily and weekly tickets available, with the Sheffield Tram & Bus Dayrider at £4.00 (adult), £2.00 (child), and £9.00 (family) offering good value for exploring the system. This ticket is also valid on Stagecoach buses throughout the Sheffield fare zone.

Key Location

The centre of the network is at Cathedral in the heart of Sheffield city centre. It features the Grade 1 listed Cathedral as an attractive backdrop. Each of the three routes pass through here, while the purple route reverses on a crossover which includes a short section of interlaced track, providing further interest and activity.

The Fleet

The operational fleet up to 2016 consisted exclusively of 25 Siemens/Duewag trams built in Dusseldorf, Germany, in 1992, and delivered in time for the opening of the Supertram system in 1994.

The trams are bi-directional, double articulated vehicles featuring four bogies with all axles powered, to cope with the demands of Sheffield's hilly terrain. The trams can accommodate

80 seated passengers (plus six additional tip up seats in wheelchair bays) and 155 standing. Two low floor areas, one in each of the outer sections, account for 40% of the passenger accommodation. These are provided with pairs of double doors on each side and are fully accessible for wheelchairs and buggies. The centre section of the trams is to a high floor layout throughout, with no doors. Originally numbered 01–25, all were painted in the South Yorkshire Supertram Ltd two-tone grey livery which gave way to Stagecoach 'stripes' after the 1997 takeover, the fleet also becoming 101–125 at this time. The fleet later received the Stagecoach Rail division livery of mainly blue with red and orange flares, and orange doors, although some cars carry advertising liveries and 120 received a special livery in 2010 to commemorate 50 years since the closure of the original Sheffield tramway system. Between 2006 and 2009, and starting with tram 115, mid-life overhauls have seen some alterations made to the internal layout and a general refresh.

*Celebrity 'Sheffield Corporation Transport' liveried 120 was involved in a collision with sister 118 during October 2015. It is seen under repair inside Nunnery depot on 25th October. **James Millington***

In preparation for the tram train trials to Rotherham, seven Citylink vehicles were ordered in 2014 from Vossloh of Valencia, Spain, with deliveries commencing in December 2015. Although essentially low floor trams, capable of operation on (and having the dual role of supplementing capacity of) the existing Supertram network, the Citylink class are to be operated as the UK's first tram trains over the converted heavy rail route to Rotherham. The Citylink class are bi-directional, double articulated vehicles featuring four bogies (three powered), and capable of dual voltage operation compatible with both Supertram's 750v DC and Network Rail's 25kv AC overhead line equipment, albeit that the route to Rotherham is expected to be electrified in line with Supertram's 750v DC supply. The tram train vehicles are 100% low floor, and can accommodate 88 seated passengers with 150 standing. In line with the requirements of operation on Network Rail infrastructure, the class are fitted with TPWS, AWS and OTMR safety systems, and are equipped with GSM-R radios. Under the British Rail

To celebrate 21 years of Supertram, 123 was decked out with window stickers of cartoon style passengers, designed by Pete McKee. It is seen here at its launch on 25th October 2015.
James Millington

(BR) TOPS system, the type are allocated class 399, this number featuring ahead of Supertram fleet numbers 201 – 207. All carry a version of the standard Stagecoach Supertram livery, and have not been required to carry the usual BR yellow end warning panel.

The arrival of the UK's first Tram Train vehicle as 399201 is delivered to Nunnery depot on 30th November 2015. **Stuart Cooke**

The Future

The tram train trials in South Yorkshire are set to have a major influence on UK transport policy. With several other potential tram train schemes around the country waiting in the wings for the results, the success or failure of the experiment is certain to be subjected to close scrutiny.

Fleet details:
25 Duewag 3-section 8-axle cars built 1992 by Siemens/Duewag, Germany
Seating: 80 (plus 6) and 155 standing
Equipment: 4 x 277kw Siemens three-phase AC motors

No.	Notes
101	
102	Reformed with 111. 1995
103	
104	
105	
106	
107	
108	
109	
110	
111	Reformed with 102. 1995
112	
113	
114	
115	
116	
117	
118	Reformed with 120. 2016
119	
120	Reformed with 118. 2015
121	
122	
123	
124	
125	

Fleet details:
7 Citylink 3-section 8-axle cars built 2014-2016 by Vossloh AG, Spain
Seating: 88 and 150 standing
Equipment: 6 x 145kw VEM

No.	Notes
399201	
399202	
399203	
399204	
399205	
399206	
399207	

London Tramlink
Croydon

Vital Statistics

Opened: 2000
Operator: London Tramlink
Number of lines: Four
Depots: Therapia Lane
Route mileage: 17 (27.3km)
Power supply: 750V DC overhead line
Track gauge: 4ft 8½in (1435mm)
Website: www.tfl.gov.uk/trams

Background

London Tramlink (originally Croydon Tramlink) opened in 2000, returning trams to the streets of London for the first time since 1952. Construction of the system included the use of former railway alignments, alignment sharing with a third rail electrified line between Birkbeck and Beckenham Junction (operated by Southern) and entirely new alignments both on and off street. The on-street section in the centre of Croydon is based on a large one-way loop, operated in a clockwise direction, which from East Croydon station traverses George Street and Church Street, before turning at Reeves Corner to travel along Tamworth Road and then back via Wellesley Road. The loop also serves as the turning circle for lines 1 and 2 which reverse here to head back to Elmers End and Beckenham Junction respectively. Connections with London Underground are available at Wimbledon (District Line), and heavy rail connections exist at Wimbledon, Mitcham Junction, West Croydon (London Overground), East Croydon, Birkbeck, Beckenham Junction and Elmers End. The depot and control centre is located at Therapia Lane on the Wimbledon route.

Tramtrack Croydon Ltd was acquired by Transport for London in June 2008, a move which saw the traditional red and white livery on the trams changed for a new lime

green, white and blue, reflecting the colours of the Tramlink routes as used by TfL on their system maps.

Since the opening of the system, changes have included an additional tram stop on the town centre loop at Centrale whilst, more recently, sections of former single line track between Mitcham and Mitcham Junction have been doubled to improve reliability on the route to and from Wimbledon. This culminated with a remodel of the terminal facilities at Wimbledon, increasing the capacity of the platforms to hold two trams simultaneously.

2555 is seen at Therapia Lane tram stop, where the system's only depot is situated. The Stadler Variobahns are very impressive looking trams and the livery suits them well. The interior layout isn't to TFL's perfect requirements, as they are an off-the-shelf product they are the most suitable currently on the market. **David Umpleby**

Routes and Services

Four services are operated as of spring 2016:

Line 1: Elmers End – East Croydon – town centre loop – East Croydon
Line 2: Beckenham Junction – East Croydon – town centre loop – East Croydon
Line 3: New Addington – East Croydon - Wimbledon
Line 4: Elmers End – East Croydon – Therapia Lane

Lines 1 and 4 combine to provide a 7/8 minute service between Elmers End and East Croydon.

Timetable

Of all the systems, Croydon operates the longest day. On a typical weekday the last tram to arrive back at Therapia Lane depot (in service) is 01.41 and the first advertised departure is 04.14 (Line 3) to New Addington. Similar to Blackpool, there are few empty stock moves, all trams are in service at all times. All trams start and finish each day at Therapia Lane depot.

Line 1: From Elmers End the first trams are: 04.55 (M-S), 07.25 (Sun) and the last tram is 01.10 (daily). First trams from East Croydon are: 04.31 (M-S), 07.01 (Sun) and the last tram is 00.46 (daily). The basic daily service is every 15 minutes all day.

Line 2: From Beckenham Junction the first trams are: 05.38 (M-S), 07.23 (Sun) and the last tram is 01.08 (daily). From East Croydon the first trams are: 05.08 (M-S), 06.53 (Sun) and the last tram is 00.38 (daily). The basic daily service is every 10 minutes during the day, every 15 minutes in the evening.

Line 3: From New Addington the first trams are: 04.50 (M-S), 06.38 (Sun) and the last tram is 01.08 (daily). From Wimbledon the first trams are: 05.39 (Mon-Sat), 07.17 (Sun) and the last tram is 00.47 (daily). The basic daily service is every 7/8 minutes during the day, every 7/8 minutes during the evening (M-F) and every 15 minutes during the evening (Sat-Sun).

Line 4: From Elmers End the first trams are: 07.18 (M-F), 08.33 (Sat), no Sunday service and the last trams are: 19.46 (M-F), 18.46 (Sat), no Sunday service. From Therapia Lane the first trams are: 06.29 (M-F), 07.44 (Sat), no Sunday service and the last trams are 19.14 (M-F), 18.14 (Sat), no Sunday service. The basic daytime service is every 15 minutes.

2542 is one of twenty four Bombardier CR4000 trams built in 1998/9 for the opening of the system. In recent years various advert designs have been applied, some being very colourful like the example seen here at Therapia Lane on 10th March 2015. The tram is advertising Turkish Airlines. The green livery underneath can be seen on the front of the tram under the fleet number, giving the impression of a green tongue sticking out! ***David Umpleby***

The hub of London Tramlink is undoubtedly East Croydon, which links with the national network. Trams can be seen operating out of here in the peak every few minutes as all the various routes have to run through here. On 15th June 2015, 2534 is seen on Service 3 to New Addington, advertising McMillan Williams Solicitors, in another attractive all-over advert.
David Umpleby

During 2015 London Tramlink, the operators of the Croydon Tramway, had a big campaign to improve public awareness of the dangers around a light rail system. This included several special postings on social media, adverts along the system and an advert tram. The car chosen was 2550, one of the CR4000 type trams, with a striking yellow advert, which is seen here negotiating the tight curve from Station Road onto the A212 heading towards Wellesley Road Tramlink Stop on its way to New Addington on Service 3. **David Umpleby**

Fares and Tickets

Single cash fares at £2.40 per journey and a £5.00 one-day bus and tram-only ticket are available from at-stop ticket machines on all platforms. With a pre-loaded TfL Oystercard, Oyster daily price cap at £6.50 offers the best value.

London Tramlink falls within Transport for London's zonal fare system, with a zone 1-6 card needed for Tramlink. A Day Anytime Travelcard costs £17.20 (£12.10 Day Off-Peak). Saturday and Sunday are off peak all day.

Key Location

East Croydon station on the town centre loop provides a three track layout through which all four services pass and can be seen as the focal point of the system. It can be a crowded location, however, making photography challenging at times. The adjacent George Street is more suitable at busy periods.

The Fleet

The 24 Bombardier Flexity Swift CR4000 trams which were supplied for the opening of the system are double articulated (with a very small centre section), bi-directional trams mounted on three bogies of which the outer two are powered. Each tram seats 70, and can accommodate 138 standing passengers. The low floor area occupies 76% of the passenger saloons, with high floor sections at each end over the powered bogies. All 24 trams were delivered in a very traditional London livery of red and white, and fleet numbers commenced at 2530, following on from the highest numbered tram on the former system in Croydon. All CR4000 trams were fitted with electronic destination screens in 2006, then, following the TfL buyout, were refurbished in 2008/9, each tram receiving a deep clean, new seating and repaints into a new lime green, white and blue livery from 2008.

To increase capacity, six Variobahn trams were ordered from Stadler Rail in Pankow, Germany, with the first delivered in January 2012. Three of these came from an order for five which had already been built to fulfil an order for Bybanen in Bergen, Norway, and were diverted to Croydon, with three purpose built for Croydon. The type entered service from March 2012. An option existed for a further eight, but in the event four more were ordered, arriving between May and December 2015. Fleet numbers are 2554 – 2563.

The Variobahns are five section, bi-directional trams mounted on three bogies and featuring two suspended sections. Each tram is 100% low floor and seats 72, with 134 standing. All cars were delivered in the new livery of lime green, white and blue, but 2554 soon received a blue based advertisement livery for 'Love Croydon' in recognition of a contribution of £3 million from the London Borough of Croydon towards the cost of these additional vehicles. The first of the second batch, 2560 carries a special 'New Trams For Croydon' livery, resembling a present being unwrapped. 2556 returned to Stadler during September 2015 for repairs to damage sustained to the roof, being redelivered to Croydon in January 2016.

New Addington in the evening summer sun on 15th June 2015. 2550 has just arrived with a service 3 from Wimbledon as 2530 waits with the next service 3 back to Wimbledon. Although New Addington is one of the most deprived parts of the network, the terminus area has a pleasant suburban feel with tree-lined roads and fields. The trams also connect with local buses here. **David Umpleby**

The Future

During 2015 Transport for London began a public consultation into a proposed new loop line between Wellesley Road and George Street on one of three proposed alignments. Other extensions have been suggested, including to Sutton (from the Wimbledon branch), but that to Crystal Palace (from Line 2, linking at Harrington Road and Beckenham) has seemed to be the most likely. However, despite being on the drawing board for some considerable time it has not been progressed, and could yet fall foul of plans to extend London Underground's Bakerloo Line into Beckenham.

Fleet details:
23 CR4000 3-section 6-axle cars built 1998-1999 by Bombardier, Austria
Seating: 70 and 138 standing
Equipment: 4 x 120kw Bombardier three phase AC motors

No.	Name
2530	
2531	
2532	
2533	
2534	
2535	Stephen Parascandolo 1980-2007
2536	
2537	
2538	
2539	
2540	
2541	
2542	
2543	
2544	
2545	
2546	
2547	
2548	
2549	
2550	
2551	
2552	
2553	

Fleet details:
10 Variobahn 5-section 6-axle cars built 2011-2012 by Stadler, Germany
Seating: 72 and 134 standing
Equipment: 8 x 45kw three phase AC motors

No.	Notes
2554	
2555	
2556	
2557	
2558	
2559	
2560	
2561	
2562	
2563	

Midland Metro
Birmingham

Vital Statistics

Opened: 1999
Operator: National Express
Number of lines: One
Depots: Wednesbury
Route mileage: 13 (21km)
Power supply: 750V DC overhead line
Track gauge: 4ft 8½in (1435mm)
Website: www.nxbus.co.uk/the-metro/

Background

Midland Metro opened its line between Birmingham and Wolverhampton in 1999. The bulk of the route reused a section of the former Great Western Railway from Snow Hill station in Birmingham, via Wednesbury (closed in 1972), but incorporating ¾ mile of new on-street alignment in Wolverhampton between Priestfield and the terminus at St. George's. The system is owned by Centro, and operated by National Express Midland Metro, a subsidiary of National Express, which also operates local bus services throughout the West Midlands area.

Until December 2015 trams occupied the former Network Rail platform 4 at Snow Hill station, which had never been seen as a satisfactory city centre terminus and had long been blamed for poorer than expected patronage on the line. Plans for the trams to escape this 'hidden' environment and take to the streets of Birmingham, where they could access a more prominent and useful terminus, began to come to fruition in June 2012 with the construction of a new on-street link between Snow Hill and New Street stations. This will hopefully be the first stage of a future extension through to Five Ways, which was the originally proposed terminus. The city centre extension diverges from the existing line between St. Paul's and Snow Hill, bypassing Snow Hill station via a new embankment/viaduct which will allow Network Rail to reinstate platform 4 for trains. Services to a new temporary terminus at Bull Street commenced during December 2015, and trams are expected to reach New Street during 2016. Approval for a further extension from Stephenson Street

WOLVERHAMPTON ST GEORGE'S
The Royal
Priestfield
The Crescent
Bilston Central
Loxdale
Bradley Lane
WEDNESBURY PARKWAY
Wednesbury, Great Western Street
Black Lake
Dudley Street, Guns Village
Dartmouth Street
Lodge Road, West Bromwich Town Hall
West Bromwich Central
Trinity Way
Kenrick Park
The Hawthorns
Handsworth, Booth Street
Winson Green, Outer Circle
Soho, Benson Road
Jewellery Quarter
St Paul's
BIRMINGHAM SNOW HILL
Bull Street
Corporation Street
Birmingham New Street — under construction (due 2016)
Town Hall
Centenary Square — under construction (due 2017)

towards Town Hall and Centenary Square, taking trams even closer to Five Ways, was granted in October 2013 and could be completed by 2017.

Routes and Services

As the system consists of just one route from Wolverhampton St. George's to Bull Street, it is operated as an end to end service with no variations. The route is known as 'line 1', a designation which will have more relevance when proposed extensions come to fruition. Trams take 36 minutes to complete a single journey and frequencies operate at up to every eight minutes. Services are expected to be extended to Corporation Street and New Street during 2016.

*At the limit of the street running section along Bilston Road, Wolverhampton, 19 awaits the signal to cross to the former railway alignment at Priestfield on 15th April 2015. **James Millington***

Timetable

From Wolverhampton the first trams are: 05.15 (M-S), 08.00 (Sun). Last trams are: 00.07 (M-F), 00.37 (Sat), 23.44 (Sun). From Bull Street the first trams are: 05.14 (M-S), 07.59 (Sun). Last trams are: 00.06 (M-F), 00.36 (Sat), 23.45 (Sun). Similar to Croydon and Blackpool there are few empty stock workings. All trams run in service to/from Wednesbury Parkway on journeys to/from depot. As a result the earliest journey on the system is 04.43 Wednesbury Parkway to Bull Street and the last arrival is at 00.59 from Bull Street (Saturdays). The basic service is: Mon-Fri - every six minutes peak, every eight minutes off peak, every 15 minutes in the evening. Saturdays: every eight minutes during the day, every 15 minutes in the evening. Sundays: every 15 minutes all day.

Fares and Tickets

Payable to conductor: Single, daily and weekly tickets available, with the Metro Daytripper at £5.00 (adult), £4.30 (child) and £10.00 (family) offering good value for exploring the system.

Key Location

Following the opening of the first portion of the city centre extension during December 2015, the street running section in the city centre towards the temporary terminus at Bull Street has become the focal point of the line. With services extending through to New Street before the end of 2016, this will give even more opportunities to capture trams in their first year back on the streets of Birmingham since the original system closed in 1953.

Trams returned to the heart of Birmingham city centre during December 2015. No.30 is seen heading for the temporary terminus at Bull Street on 3rd February 2016. **James Millington**

The Fleet

The operational fleet is made up exclusively of CAF Urbos 3 trams, built at Beasain in Spain, and delivered between 2013 and 2015.

The Urbos 3 trams are bi-directional, five section articulated vehicles mounted on three bogies, and accomodate over 200 passengers (52 seated). Specification is 100% low floor and they have been delivered in the new standard white, silver and magenta livery. Originally planned to number 20 vehicles in total, a 21st was ordered during 2014, and fleet numbers 17 to 37 are allocated. Deliveries commenced in October 2013 and were completed in March 2015; the type entering service from September 2014.

Midland Metro's original fleet consisted of 16 Ansaldo Firema T69 type light rail vehicles numbered 01 – 016 and delivered for the opening of the line in 1999. These soon proved to be too small to cope with loadings, and developed a reputation for unreliability with several examples spending considerable periods out of use. 01 and 02 were the first to be withdrawn, and were progressively joined by further members of the fleet in a process which was stepped up during 2014/15 as the Urbos 3s gradually took over. 016 became the final T69 to operate in public service, in August 2015. 014 was the first to depart the premises when it was transferred to secure storage at Long Marston, Warwickshire, in June 2014. It has been joined by several others, with all of the type expected to eventually move into storage pending possible (but seemingly unlikely) potential use on future extensions.

Tram 26 arrives at the island platform at Bradley Lane on 15th April 2015. **James Millington**

The Future

In November 2013 it was announced that consideration was being given to the construction of a Midland Metro 'Line 2', from Birmingham city centre to Coventry via Birmingham International Airport. The motivation was to give both Birmingham and Coventry better access to the proposed HS2 station at Curzon Street, and further consultation has recently been held regarding the possibility of extending this through Digbeth. Funding for the first phase of this 'Eastside Extension' was secured during February 2014, which will take trams via either Moor

Street or Albert Street, and Curzon Street, before reaching a new terminus at Adderley Street, with completion expected in 2021.

During March 2014 a long awaited extension at the Wolverhampton end of the line was finally announced. This is basically a cut down version of a long standing larger scale plan to create a loop around Wolverhampton town centre. The new line will continue from the current terminus at St. George's, serving two new stops at Piper's Row (for the bus station) and Wolverhampton railway station. Work will hopefully be completed by 2019.

Bilston Road in Wolverhampton is the setting for this view of tram 21, seen heading towards the terminus at St. George's on 15th April 2015. **James Millington**

A further extension, from Wednesbury to Merry Hill via Dudley, would involve conversion of the former South Staffordshire Line through Tipton. A business plan for this was submitted to Network Rail during 2011 but no timescales for construction have been set.

Tram 16 was the last of the T69 class to run in service, during August 2015. Prior to this, on 15th April 2015, the tram heads towards Birmingham at Wednesbury Great Western Street. **James Millington**

Operational fleet:
21 Urbos 3 5-section 6-axle cars built 2013-2015 by CAF, Spain
Seating: 52 (plus 2) and 154 standing
Equipment: 12 x 80kw motors

No.	Name	Notes
17		
18		
19		
20		
21		
22		
23		
24		
25		
26		
27		
28		
29		
30		
31		
32		
33		
34		
35	Angus Adams	
36		
37		

Stored fleet:
10 T69 3-section 6-axle cars built 1996-1999 by Ansaldo Firema, Italy
Seating: 52 (plus 4) and 102 standing
Equipment: 4 x 105kw motors

No.	Name	Notes
04	Sir Frank Whittle	
05	Sister Dora	
06	Alan Garner	
09	Jeff Astle	Reformed with 010. 2006
12		
16	Gerwyn John	

Note: Withdrawn trams 01, 02, 03, 07, 08, 10, 11, 13, 14 and 15 have been transferred to Long Marston for further storage.

Nottingham Express Transit

Vital Statistics

Opened: 2004
Operator: Nottingham Trams Ltd
Number of lines: Two
Depots: Wilkinson Street
Route mileage: 20 (32km)
Power supply: 750V DC overhead line
Track gauge: 4ft 8½in (1435mm)
Website: www.thetram.net

Background

Phase 1 of the Nottingham Express Transit (NET) system opened in 2004 connecting Nottingham railway station with Hucknall, eight miles to the north, plus a short branch to a park and ride facility at Phoenix Park. Much of the system provided a brand new, mainly on-street, alignment featuring mixed and segregated running. However, north of the tram depot at Wilkinson Street and thence all the way to Hucknall, the tramway shares an alignment with (but is separate from) Network Rail's Robin Hood line. North of Bulwell, both railway and tramway are reduced to a single track (with passing loops for NET at Bulwell Forest, Moor Bridge and Butler's Hill) due to the narrow alignment of the trackbed.

Originally operated by the Nottingham Tram Consortium, which is a joint initiative between Transdev and Nottingham City Transport, a re-tendering process in advance of the expansion of the system led to the Tramlink Nottingham consortium, which includes local bus operator Trent Barton) taking control from December 2011. Nottingham Trams Ltd operate and maintain the system on behalf of Tramlink Nottingham.

Construction of Phase 2, which was to take trams in the opposite direction from the original stub terminus at Nottingham station on two separate lines towards Clifton and

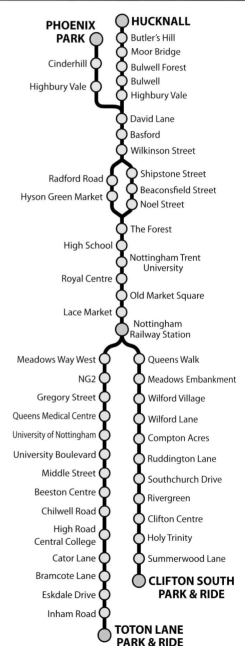

Toton Lane, began in 2012. When they opened in August 2015, the extensions more than doubled the size of the tramway at a stroke, and a combined fleet of 37 trams now provide an intensive service across the expanded network.

*The focal point of the Nottingham system is Old Market Square, where Incentro trams 201 and 205 are seen passing on 2nd September 2015. **James Millington***

Routes and Services

Although not designated as such, NET uses the line colours of purple and green:

Purple: Phoenix Park – David Lane - Nottingham Station – Toton Lane

Green: Hucknall – David Lane - Nottingham Station – Clifton South

Timetable

Purple line: From Phoenix Park the first tram is 06.04 daily. Mondays to Fridays the service is then every 15 minutes until 07.03; every seven minutes until 10.10; every 10 minutes until 15.02; every seven minutes until 19.10; every 10 minutes until 21.02 then every 15 minutes until 00.15. On Saturdays the service is every 15 minutes until 07.18; every 10 minutes until 10.17; every 7 minutes until 19.10; every 10 minutes until 21.02 then every 15 minutes until 00.15. On Sundays, the service is every 15 minutes until 07.02; every 10 minutes until 19.02 and every 15 minutes until 23.15. From Clifton South, the first tram is 06.02 (daily) and the service operates at almost identical times to above with the last tram 00.48 (M-S), 23.48 (Sun).

Green Line: From Hucknall the first tram is 06.04 daily. The frequency patterns are almost identical to the purple line daily, with the last tram at 00.15 (M-S) and 23.15 (Sun). From Toton Lane the first tram is 06.01 (daily) and again service levels are almost identical daily, with the last tram at 01.05 (M-S), 00.05 (Sun). Trams on both routes start and finish each day at Wilkinson Street depot.

Incentro 208 arrives at Wilford Lane on 4th February 2016 with a service for Clifton South. **James Millington**

Fares and Tickets

At stop ticket machines: Single, daily and weekly tickets available, with day tickets at £4.00 (adult), £2.20 (child) and £9.00 (Peak Group) offering good value for exploring the system.

Key Location

Although the city centre offers an attractive setting for the tramway, particularly at Old Market Square where Nottingham's Grade II listed Council House forms an impressive backdrop, the three track layout at The Forest offers a quieter location to record the trams away from the hordes of pedestrians who are ever present in the city centre. Both services pass through The Forest, which offers a wide segregation away from road traffic and with weekday daytime frequencies of up to every 3 minutes in each direction, there is always plenty of activity here.

The Fleet

Until 2014, all services were provided by the original fleet of 15 Incentro AT6/5 trams built by ABB Transportation at Derby (more commonly known as Adtranz) in 2003/4. By the time construction began, Bombardier Transportation had acquired Adtranz and taken over the Derby factory, so the trams were actually supplied by Bombardier but to the Adtranz design. Nottingham's Incentro trams are 100% low floor (the first such in the UK). The trams are five section bi-directional cars supported on three bogies. Each vehicle seats 54, plus 8 additional seats in wheelchair bays and perch seats, and can accommodate 129 standing. The original livery of dark green, silver and black was applied (although Nottingham has made considerable use of full vinyl advertising wraps over the years). However, from March 2013, and starting with last built 215, a refresh programme has seen all cars pass through the workshops for attention including new seat coverings and LED internal lighting. A brighter livery of silver and green was subsequently adopted, with the original colours eradicated by December 2013.

*Citadis 236 approaches the new terminus at Toton Lane on 4th February 2016. **James Millington***

Wilford Toll Bridge is the setting for Citadis 232, seen crossing the River Trent with a service for Clifton South on 4th February 2016. **James Millington**

For the Phase 2 expansion, 22 Citadis 302 trams were ordered from Alstom and constructed at their Barcelona factory. The Citadis vehicles are five section bi-directional trams supported on three bogies. Each vehicle seats 62 and accommodates 138 standing. The first of the type, 216, was delivered to NET's Wilkinson Street depot in September 2013 wearing the new livery of silver and green; deliveries were completed by the arrival of 237 in November 2014. Five of the new trams were put to use from mid-2014 to provide capacity enhancements on Phase 1, with others gradually joining the operational ranks up to the opening of the Phase 2 extensions in August 2015.

Both types of tram are used across the expanded system.

Incentro 209, wearing an in-house advertising livery for NET, ascends the southern ramp of Wilford Toll Bridge on 4th February 2016. **James Millington**

Fleet details:
15 Incentro AT6/5 5-section 6-axle cars built 2002-2003 by Bombardier Transportation, Derby
Seating: 54 (plus 4) and 129 standing
Equipment: 8 x 45kw motors

No.	Name	No.	Name
201	Torvill and Dean	209	Sid Standard
202	D H Lawrence	210	Sir Jesse Boot
203	William "Bendigo" Thompson	211	Robin Hood
204	Erica Beardsmore	212	William Booth
205	Lord Byron	213	Mary Potter
206	Angela Alcock	214	Dennis McCarthy, MBE
207	Mavis Worthington	215	Brian Clough
208	Dinah Minton		

Fleet details:
22 Citadis 302 5-section 6-axle cars built 2012-2013 by Alstom, Barcelona
Seating: 62 and 138 standing
Equipment: 6 x 120kw motors

No.	Name	No.	Name
216	Julie Poulter	227	Sir Peter Mansfield
217	Carl Froch MBE	228	Local Armed Forces Heroes
218	Jim Taylor	229	Viv Anderson MBE
219	Alan Sillitoe	230	George Green
220	Kim Helm	231	
221	Stephen Lowe	232	William Ivory
222	Barbara White OBE	233	Ada Lovelace
223	Colin Slater MBE	234	George Africanus
224	Vicky McClure	235	David Clarke
225		236	Sat Bains
226	Jimmy Sirrel and Jack Wheeler	237	Stuart Broad

The Future

In December 2014 Broxtowe Borough Council declined to fund a feasibility study into a line to Kimberley. Following the opening of the current extensions there are no plans for further expansion despite nine possible routes being highlighted during the tender process for phase two. However, the possible siting of a future station for HS2 at Toton, just a short distance from Chilwell, could see a spur added to serve this at some point in the future.

Edinburgh Trams

Vital Statistics

Opened: 2014
Operator: Edinburgh Trams Ltd
Number of lines: One
Depot: Gogar
Route mileage: 8.7 (14km)
Power supply: 750V DC overhead line
Track gauge: 4ft 8½in (1435mm)
Website: www.edinburghtrams.com

Background

The current line between York Place and Edinburgh Airport is only part of what was planned to be a much larger network to be delivered for £375m, but contractual disputes and escalating costs saw the project scaled back in a bid to salvage something from the original plans. Although construction began in June 2008, as late as 2011 there was still serious debate about scrapping the entire scheme, for which costs were approaching £800m and all 27 trams had already been built. However, it was decided to continue with the project but only between the Airport and St. Andrews Square, latterly extended the short distance to York Place, in the city centre. Following completion and testing, the tramway finally opened to the public in May 2014, having been delivered within its revised budget of £776m, but the eight mile line is a shadow of what was originally proposed to also serve Leith, Newhaven and Granton.

EDINBURGH AIRPORT

Ingliston Park & Ride

Gogarburn

Edinburgh Gateway
under construction

Gyle Centre

Edinburgh Park Central

EDINBURGH PARK STATION

Bankhead

Saughton

Balgreen

Murrayfield Stadium

HAYMARKET

West End - Princes Street

Princes Street

ST. ANDREW SQUARE

YORK PLACE

Routes and Services

The system consists of just one route from York Place to Edinburgh Airport which is operated as an end to end service with no variations, taking 40 minutes. The operation is co-ordinated with the Lothian Buses network under the new umbrella of Transport for Edinburgh.

251 heads towards Edinburgh Airport at Saughton on 12th February 2015. James Millington

Timetable

The Edinburgh timetable is very simple. Daily, the first tram is 05.00 from Gyle Centre (the first stop out of Gogar depot) to York Place. It works the 05.29 to the Airport, then the 06.15 back to York Place. Monday to Saturday, the service is then at least every 10 minutes for an hour then every 8-10 minutes for the rest of the day. On Sundays there is a basic 12-15 minute service all day. The timetable finishes the same daily, with a 22.45 from Airport to York Place, a 23.08 York Place to Airport, followed by 23.18 and 23.28 from York Place as far as Gyle Centre. A Sunday service normally operates on Bank Holidays. It is noted that the 05.00 start is by far the earliest Sunday journey on any UK light rail system. Note: Empty stock workings are not detailed, but all trams start and finish each day at Gogar depot.

Fares and Tickets

At stop ticket machines on all platforms: Single, return and period tickets are available. The Dayticket – City Zone at £4.00 (adult), £2.00 (child) and £8.50 (family) includes all stops except Edinburgh Airport; The Dayticket – Airport Zone at £9.00 (adult) and £4.50 (child) includes the airport stop. Both tickets are also valid on Lothian Bus services.

Key location

Princes Street in Edinburgh offers the best and most picturesque location to see the trams, but has the disadvantage that the tramway occupies a central location in the roadway which can make photographing the lengthy trams challenging. A better place for photography is the short section between the junction of Princes Street with South St. Andrew Street, and the tram stop at St. Andrew Square. This is segregated from other road traffic and often much clearer of pedestrians.

*With the city of Edinburgh in the background, 265 prepares to cross over the railway line at Saughton on 30th October 2014. **James Millington***

*Tram 271 leaves the highway for roadside reservation at Edinburgh Haymarket on 12th February 2015. **James Millington***

The Fleet

The fleet is made up exclusively of 27 bespoke vehicles produced by CAF in Beasain, Spain. The trams are seven section, bi-directional 100% low floor trams mounted on four bogies. Each vehicle seats 78 and can accommodate 170 standing passengers. Despite several livery trials before the system commenced operation, a traditional livery of madder, white (officially Weinrot und Weiss) and silver was adopted during 2013, when the operation was rebranded 'Edinburgh Trams'.

The depot at Gogar, as seen on 30th October 2014. 262, then still in non-standard livery (along with 269), is seen in the background. **James Millington**

The Future

Following the opening of the tramway during 2014, Edinburgh City Council commissioned a report on the feasibility of potential tram extensions. These chiefly examined three potential options to extend the tramway from York Place to the Foot of Leith Walk, continuing to Ocean Terminal and thence to Newhaven as per the original plans, at a projected cost of £144.7m.

Fleet details:
27 7-section 8-axle cars built 2009-2011 by CAF, Spain
Seating: 78 and 170 standing
Equipment: 12 x 80kw motors

No.	Notes	No.	Notes
251		265	
252		266	
253		267	
254		268	
255		269	
256		270	
257		271	
258		272	
259		273	
260		274	
261		275	
262		276	
263		277	
264			

Blackpool Tramway

Vital Statistics

Opened: 1885
Operator: Blackpool Transport
Number of lines: One
Depots: Starr Gate and Rigby Road
Route mileage: 11.5 (18.5km)
Power supply: 600V DC overhead line
Track gauge: 4ft 8½in (1435mm)
Website: www.blackpooltransport.com

Background

The Blackpool tramway opened in September 1885 as the first electric street tramway in Britain. By coincidence, it was also to become the only commercial tramway on the UK mainland to survive the wholesale demise of this mode of transport in the years up to 1962.

The tramway expanded greatly between 1895 and 1902, and was enlarged by the purchase of the neighbouring Blackpool and Fleetwood Electric Tramroad in 1920. The closure of street routes began in 1936 and was completed between 1961 and 1963, leaving the line as it is today. The current route consists of four miles of surviving Corporation tramway from Starr Gate to Gynn Square, and a further seven miles of the old Tramroad route from here to Fleetwood. The tramway is owned by Blackpool Council and operated by Blackpool Transport Services Ltd, an 'arm's length' company owned by the Council.

Following the completion of a £100m upgrade in 2012, the Blackpool tramway became the only UK system to make the transition from first generation tramway to second generation light rail system. All timetabled services are handled by 16 Bombardier built Flexity2 trams, which are housed at a purpose built depot at Starr Gate.

Heritage Operations

In recognition of Blackpool's long tramway history, a representative selection of heritage and illuminated feature trams were retained following the tramway upgrade to provide heritage and illuminations tours, principally throughout the tourist season. The heritage fleet is based at the surviving Rigby Road depot, which was the main operational base for the tramway from 1935 to 2011.

FLEETWOOD FERRY
Victoria Street
London Street
Fisherman's Walk
Stanley Road
Lindel Road
Heathfield Road
Broadwater
Rossall Square
Rossall School
Rossall Beach
Thornton Gate
West Drive
CLEVELEYS
Anchorsholme Lane
Little Bispham
Norbreck North*   *Opening
                    Easter 2016
Norbreck
Sandhurst Avenue
BISPHAM
Cavendish Road
Lowther Avenue
Cabin
Cliffs Hotel
Gynn Square
Wilton Parade
Pleasant Street
NORTH PIER
Tower
Central Pier
Manchester Square
St Chad's Road
Waterloo Road
South Pier
PLEASURE BEACH
Burlington Road West
Harrow Place
STARR GATE

Flexity2 016 is the only one of its type in Blackpool so far to carry all over advertising. This is the second design carried for 'Freeport Fleetwood', as seen on 9th April 2015. **James Millington**

Routes and Services

The year round Starr Gate to Fleetwood service is operated by the Bombardier Flexity2 trams at up to every 10 minutes during the summer and up to every 15 minutes during the winter. This is supplemented during busy periods of the summer season and autumn illuminations by a small fleet of rebuilt 1930s vehicles which operate as unscheduled 'specials', being directed around the system as required.

Starting prior to Easter, heritage services operate at weekends, and on weekdays during school holidays, throughout the season. The core heritage service runs between Pleasure Beach and North Pier, with selected journeys extended to Cabin, using two heritage trams. Gold heritage weekends (which include bank holiday weekends) feature up to six different heritage trams each day and include tours to Fleetwood. During the autumn illuminations, tours operate from dusk every evening, departing from Pleasure Beach. The heritage fleet is available for private hire at all times, and enquiries should be made to heritage.trams@blackpooltransport.com

Timetable

Due to the seasonal variation in passenger numbers, the Blackpool system usually operates four timetables a year. The winter service commences at the end of the Illuminations in early November and ends pre-Easter. A basic 15 minute timetable operates over the whole route daily, every 30 minutes in the evening. A spring service runs from Easter until late June/early July, with a basic 12 minute headway during the day daily, and then every 30 minutes Starr Gate - Bispham and every 30 minutes Starr Gate - Fleetwood, during the evening, to give a 15 minute promenade service. The summer service usually operates from late June/early July until the end of August, providing a 10 minute daytime service daily and the same 30/30

Balloon 715 and Standard 147 are captured together at Pleasure Beach whilst operating heritage tours on 23rd May 2015. *James Millington*

minute service in the evening. During the Illuminations, usually late August/early September until early November, a 10 or 12 minute daytime service operates during the day daily and with departures every 7/8 or 10 minutes from Starr Gate in the evening. Two trams per hour run to Fleetwood, the rest terminate at Bispham. Generally, year round, the first tram is 05.00 Starr Gate to Fleetwood weekdays, 06.00 Saturdays and 07.00 Sundays. The last tram is 00.15 Fleetwood to Starr Gate, daily. A Saturday service normally operates on Bank Holidays. Blackpool is the only UK system which does not increase capacity during morning/evening peaks. There are no empty stock workings. All trams are in service at all times (except for reverse moves at Starr Gate, Bispham etc).

Fares and Tickets

Payable to conductor: Single, daily, weekly and monthly tickets available, with the Blackpool1 ticket at £5.00 (adult), £2.50 (child) and £10.00 (family) offering good value for exploring the system (also valid on all BTS bus services). These can be purchased online in advance or at any PayPoint store for a discount. Heritage day tickets are available from any conductor (or bus driver), at £10.00 (adult) and £6.00 (child), and are valid on all tram and bus services operated by BTS.

'B' fleet Balloon 711 seen at Manchester Square on 7th May 2015, whilst unusually allocated to a timetabled working to Starr Gate. **James Millington**

Key Location

The focal point of the tramway throughout its history has been at Talbot Square (North Pier), where a number of town routes met the Promenade tramway in the years prior to 1962. Despite the reduction in scale of the tramway and the reversal facilities at North Pier, which lost its lengthy three track layout in 2011 (replaced by a shorter passing loop located slightly to the south), the significance of this location is set to increase again in the years to come once the planned extension to Blackpool North railway station has been completed.

The Fleet

The year round operation is provided by 16 Bombardier Flexity2 trams, numbered 001 – 016, supplied as part of the tramway upgrade and launched into service from Easter 2012. The bi-directional trams are 100% low floor and feature five sections mounted on three 'Flexx Urban 3000' bogies of which the outer two are powered. Each tram seats 74, and can accommodate 148 standing passengers. Ownership of the vehicles remains with Blackpool Council, and the trams carry their purple, black and white livery rather than Blackpool Transport's yellow and black fleet livery.

Nine double deck cars, part of a batch of 27 similar trams built in the 1930s by English Electric at Preston, have been retained for continued operation to form a B fleet for use at times of peak demand. The nine cars have all received some level of refurbishment over the past 20 years, and as part of the requirements of the upgrade have been fitted with widened centre entrance platforms, driver operated power doors, and a CCTV system. Partial derogation has been granted from DfT for these cars to be used alongside the Flexity2 trams to supplement the timetabled service, as required.

Heritage fleet 'Twin car' 675+685 at Pleasure Beach on 10th October 2015. The curious orange painted trolley tower is accurate for the 1960s era represented by the tram. **James Millington**

The illuminated warship 'HMS Blackpool', is a favourite of the autumn illuminations. Seen here loading a private party from the nearby Hilton Hotel on 3rd October 2015. **James Millington**

A selection of heritage and illuminated feature cars have been retained (and some re-acquired after periods in private ownership) for use to acknowledge Blackpool's long tramway history. These trams, designated the C fleet, have received derogation from the DfT for continued operation on duties other than the provision of stage carriage services. In their new role, the operational examples see frequent use on heritage and illuminations tours and are available for private hire.

The Future

During 2014 it was announced that Blackpool Council would support the long awaited extension of the tramway from North Pier to North Station, which requires a £1.8m local contribution. This follows the allocation from Transport for Lancashire of £16.4m towards the £18.2m total cost of the extension, agreed in September 2013, and will hopefully see integration between tramway and railway restored by 2017.

In December 2014 it was revealed that a £160,000 project, jointly funded by Lancashire County Council and Sintropher, a European Union project to improve local and regional transport in Europe, was investigating the possibility of extending the tram system south towards to St. Annes. This would use the tracks of the current south Fylde railway line, and return trams to St. Annes for the first time since 1937.

A fleet:
16 Flexity2 5-section 6-axle cars built 2011-2012 by Bombardier, Germany
Seating: 74 and 148 standing
Equipment: 4 x 120kw motors

No.	Name	Notes
001		
002	Alderman E.E. Wynne	
003		
004		
005		
006		
007	Alan Whitbread	
008		
009		
010		
011		
012		
013		
014		
015		
016		

B fleet:
9 EE Balloon 4-axle bogie double deck cars built 1934-1935 by English Electric, Preston
Seating: 52 or 54 upper deck and 40 lower deck
Equipment: 2 x 40kw motors

No.	Name	Notes
700		
707		Stored
709		Stored
711	Ray Roberts	
713		
718		Stored
719	Donna's Dream House	
720		Stored
724		Stored

Works fleet

No.	Built	By	Type	Notes
260	1973*	Blackpool Corporation	Flat bed rail crane	Stored
750	1907	Fleetwood Tramroad Co.	Reel wagon	
754	1992	East Lancs	Engineering car	
939	2003#	Mercedes	Mercedes Unimog	
Crab	2012	Depot Rail	Remote control shunter	

* Indicates date rebuilt from earlier car. # Indicates date into service with BTS.

C fleet:
Various. Retained heritage trams for tours/special occasions

No.	Built	By	Name/Notes
8	1974*	Blackpool Corporation	Stored
31	1901	Blackpool Corporation	On loan from Beamish Museum
40	1914	Dick Kerr	On loan from National Tramway Museum
43	1924	English Electric	Stored
66	1901	ER&TCC	On loan from Bolton 66 Tramcar Trust
143	1924	Blackpool Corporation	Under restoration
147	1924	Hurst Nelson	'Michael Airey'/On loan to Beamish Museum
227	1934	English Electric	
230	1934	English Electric	'George Formby OBE'
259	1937	Brush	Stored
272	1960*	English Electric	
T2	1960	Metro Cammell	
279	1935	English Electric	Stored
290	1937	Brush	Stored
304	1952	Charles Roberts	Stored
600	1934	English Electric	'Duchess of Cornwall'
631	1937	Brush	
632	1937	Brush	Stored
634	1937	Brush	Stored
642	1986	East Lancs	
648	1985	East Lancs	
660	1953	Charles Roberts	Stored
663	1953	Charles Roberts	Stored
671	1960*	English Electric	Stored
681	1960	Metro Cammell	Stored
675	1958*	English Electric	
685	1960	Metro Cammell	
676	1958*	English Electric	Stored
686	1960	Metro Cammell	Stored
701	1934	English Electric	
704	1934	English Electric	Stored
706	1934	English Electric	'Princess Alice'/Stored
715	1935	English Electric	
717	1935	English Electric	'Walter Luff'
723	1935	English Electric	
732	1961*	Blackpool Corporation	Stored
733	1962*	Blackpool Corporation	Rebuilt in 2009 with parts from 677
734	1928	English Electric	
F736	2004*	Blackpool Transport	'HMS Blackpool'
737	2001*	Blackpool Transport	
761	1979*	Blackpool Corporation	Stored

* Indicates date rebuilt from earlier car. # Indicates date into service with BTS.

Dublin Luas

Vital Statistics

Opened: 2004
Operator: Veolia Transport
Number of lines: Two
Depots: Red Cow (Red Line) and Sandyford (Green Line)
Route mileage: 24 (38.6km)
Power supply: 750V DC overhead line
Track gauge: 4ft 8½in (1435mm)
Website: www.luas.ie

Background

The Dublin Luas system currently consists of two unconnected lines, the Green Line and the Red Line. Both opened in 2004 (June and September respectively), and both have subsequently been extended. The original Green Line ran from St. Stephen's Green in the city centre, to Sandyford, re-using much of the route of the former Harcourt Street railway, but with a new on street alignment between Charlemont and St. Stephen's Green. The Green Line depot is at Sandyford, beyond which the line was extended to Bride's Glen in 2010 on a completely new alignment.

The Red Line's original route ran from Connolly station in the city to Tallaght, and features a depot at Red Cow. The Red Line was extended into the eastern Docklands area in December 2009 and now terminates at The Point. This extension bypasses the original Connolly station terminus, although it remains in use as a spur from Busáras. At the other end of the line, the intermediate stop at Belgard became a junction from July 2011 with the opening of the 'Citywest' route to Saggart.

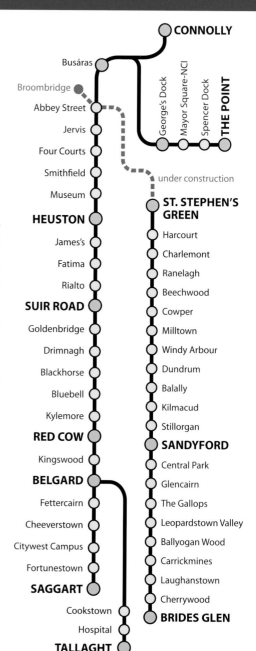

The Red Line terminus in the eastern docklands is at The Point, where 4008 awaits departure to Tallaght on 2nd July 2015. **James Millington**

Routes and Services

Two unconnected services are operated:

Green Line: St. Stephen's Green – Sandyford – Brides Glen

Red Line: Saggart/Tallaght – Belgard – Busáras – Connolly/The Point

Timetable

Red line: On weekdays, trams from Saggart operate every 9-10 minutes during peak times and every 10-15 minutes off peak. Trams from Tallaght operate every 4-10 minutes during peak times and every 10-15 minutes off peak. These two routes join up at Belgard where during the peak there is a tram every 3-5 minutes towards Busáras and every 6-15 minutes off peak. From Busáras to The Point, trams are every 4-10 minutes in the peak and every 10-15 minutes off peak. The single stop Connolly branch has a tram every 9-10 minutes peak, every 10 minutes off peak. The branch closes at 19.00. Weekend services are broadly similar, every 10-12 minutes from both Saggart and Tallaght in the peak and every 12-15 minutes from each off peak. These merge to give a 6-7 minute peak service from Belgard to Busáras on Saturdays, 6-15 minute off peak and a 10-11 minute service on Sundays peak, every 10-15 minutes off peak. From Busáras to The Point, trams are every 10-12 or 12 minutes on weekends during the peak, 11-15 or 12-15 off peak. The branch to Connolly has a limited service every 12 minutes from 09.00 to 19.00 on Saturdays and every 20 minutes, 15.00 to 19.00 on Sundays. The first tram from each terminus is: Saggart - 05.40 (M-F); 06.40 (Sat); 07.10 (Sun). Tallaght - 05.30 (M-F); 06.30 (Sat); 07.00 (Sun). The Point - 05.30 (M-F); 06.30 (Sat); 07.00 (Sun). Connolly - 07.10 (M-F); 09.05 (Sat); 15.10 (Sun). The last tram from each terminus is: Saggart - 23.50 (M-F); 23.50 (Sat); 22.50 (Sun). Tallaght - 00.00 (M-F); 00.00 (Sat); 23.00 (Sun). The Point - 00.30 (M-F); 00.30

Green Line Citadis 5011, in advertising livery for Eircom, crosses the William Dargan Bridge at Dundrum en-route to the city on 4th July 2014. **James Millington**

(Sat); 23.30 (Sun). Connolly - 19.30 (M-F); 18.50 (Sat); 19.00 (Sun). A Sunday service normally operates on Bank Holidays. Note: Empty stock workings are not detailed, but all trams will start and finish each day at Red Cow depot.

Green Line: On weekdays, services from St Stephen's Green as far as Sandyford operate every 3-6 minutes in the peak and every 6-15 minutes off peak. Some of these are extended to Brides Glen at a frequency of every 4-10 minutes in the peak, every 10-15 minutes off peak. On Saturdays, trams between St Stephen's Green and Sandyford are every 7-10 minutes in the peak and 10-15 minutes off peak and on Sundays, every 11-12 minutes in the peak, 12-15 minutes off peak. In the Sandyford - Brides Glen section, trams are every 13-15 minutes Saturdays peak, 15 minutes off peak and every 11-12 minutes Sundays peak, 12-15 minutes off peak. The first trams from each terminus are: St Stephen's Green - 05.30 (M-F); 06.30 (Sat); 07.00 (Sun). Brides Glen - 05.30 (M-F); 06.30 (Sat); 07.00 (Sun). Sandyford (towards St Stephen's Green) - 05.35 (M-F); 06.35 (Sat); 07.10 (Sun) and Sandyford (towards Brides Glen) - 05.45 (M-F); 06.30 (Sat); 07.00 (Sun). The last trams from each terminus are: St Stephen's Green - 00.30 (M-F); 00.30 (Sat); 23.30 (Sun). Brides Glen - 00.00 (M-F); 00.00 (Sat); 23.00 (Sun); Sandyford (towards St Stephen's Green) - 00.15 (M-F); 00.15 (Sat), 23.15 (Sun) and Sandyford (towards Brides Glen) - 00.45 (M-F); 00.45 (Sat); 23.45 (Sun). A Sunday service normally operates on Bank Holidays. Note: Empty stock workings are not detailed, but all trams start and finish each day at Sandyford depot.

*The junction of the Red Line branches to Tallaght and Saggart is at Belgard, where a comprehensive covered stop is provided. 3004 calls on its way to Saggart on 3rd July 2015. **James Millington***

Red Line 4009 prepares to reverse at Tallaght on 3rd July 2015. **James Millington**

Fares and Tickets

At-stop ticket machines on all platforms: Single, daily and weekly tickets available, with the Luas Flexi ticket at €6.80 (adult) and €2.80 (child) offering good value for exploring the system.

Key Location

Green Line: The impressive cable-stayed William Dargan Bridge at Dundrum, required to span the large road intersection beneath, is the undoubted focal point of the Green Line and provides an interesting backdrop for photographs.

Red Line: The area around Heuston station, adjacent to the bridge over the River Liffey, is a key location on this route. Heuston features a three track layout with a centre stub reversing road, allowing trams to reverse and return to Connolly/The Point.

The Fleet

The trams were ordered in July 1999 from Alstom and were manufactured at La Rochelle in France. For the Red Line, 26 Citadis 301 cars were acquired. These are double articulated, bi-directional trams mounted on three bogies offering a low floor area of 70%. The Red Line cars were numbered in the 3000 series, from 3001-3026. The Green Line received 14 Citadis 401 cars, which are five section bi-directional trams mounted on four bogies and also offering 70% low floor area, and these were numbered in the 4000s, from 4001-4014. Between 2007 and 2008, the Red Line cars were extended by two sections each, bringing them up to the same specification as the 4000 series cars, with the work to extend the trams taking place in-house at Red Cow depot. Route extensions and heavy loadings saw a further 26 Citadis cars delivered in 2009/10. These 5000 series cars (5001-5026) are 100% low floor and are longer still, at seven sections and 43 metres, and feature a restyled front end with a more pronounced 'nose' profile, designed to deter joyriders. The 5000 series cars were delivered to the Green Line, with the 4000 series cars cascaded to the Red Line to join 3001-3026.

The Green Line terminus at Brides Glen was still largely undeveloped when seen on 4th July 2014, with 5023 in attendance. **James Millington**

The Future

Following consultations begun in 2005 regarding a city centre 'link-up' between the two lines, work has begun which will ultimately see an extension from the Green Line terminus at St. Stephen's Green, following a new corridor serving central businesses and tourist destinations, to Broombridge, crossing the current Red Line at Abbey Street. The first major civil engineering project has seen the construction of a new bridge to carry southbound trams over the River Liffey (northbound trams will use the existing O'Connell Street bridge). The route north will reuse part of the abandoned Old Broadstone railway to minimise costs, with completion expected in 2017. The extended Green Line is expected to continue to operate separately from the Red Line, although connections will be added between the two lines to aid stock transfer between routes. Seven new trams are to be purchased for the Broombridge extension. Despite other proposals for extensions, including to Bray (from Cherrywood on the Green Line) and Lucan (from Blackhorse on the Red Line), the Government's 2012-2016 Infrastructure and Capital Investment plan contains no provision for funding further Luas extensions.

Fleet details:
26 Citadis 301 5-section 8-axle cars built 2003-2004 by Alstom, France
Seating: 72 (plus 8 tip up and 8 perch) and 220 standing
Equipment: 6 x 120kw motors   *(Delivered as 3-section cars and extended between 2007-2008)*

No.	Notes	No.	Notes
3001		3014	
3002		3015	
3003		3016	
3004		3017	
3005		3018	
3006		3019	
3007		3020	
3008		3021	
3009		3022	
3010		3023	
3011		3024	
3012		3025	
3013		3026	

Fleet details:
14 Citadis 301 5-section 8-axle cars built 2003-2004 by Alstom, France
Seating: 72 (plus 8 tip up and 8 perch) and 220 standing
Equipment: 6 x 120kw motors   *(Delivered as 3-section cars and extended between 2007-2008)*

No.	Notes	No.	Notes
4001		4008	
4002		4009	
4003		4010	
4004		4011	
4005		4012	
4006		4013	
4007		4014	

Fleet details:
26 Citadis 402 7-section 8-axle cars built 2009-2010 by Alstom, France
Seating: 68 (plus 8) and 291 standing
Equipment: 6 x 120kw motors

No.	Notes	No.	Notes
5001		5014	
5002		5015	
5003		5016	
5004		5017	
5005		5018	
5006		5019	
5007		5020	
5008		5021	
5009		5022	
5010		5023	
5011		5024	
5012		5025	
5013		5026	

Heritage

Manx Electric Railway
Isle of Man

Vital Statistics

Opened: 1893
Operator: Isle of Man Government (Isle of Man Railways)
Number of lines: One
Depots: Derby Castle and Laxey (Ramsey - closed)
Route mileage: 17.75 (28.5km)
Power supply: 550V DC overhead line
Track gauge: 3ft (915mm)
Website: www.gov.im/publictransport

Background

The Isle of Man Tramways & Electric Power Co Ltd opened a line from Douglas (Derby Castle) to Groudle in 1893 (2.25 miles), a simple single track line with passing loops. The service started on 07/09/1893 and ceased after only 19 days! Electric traction was in its pioneering days and everything was a learning curve. Plans to use one motor and two trailers were soon realised to be optimistic, one trailer being used thereafter. The line initially opened with overhead wires using Hopkinson bow collectors (as seen on the Snaefell Mountain Railway). The success of the opening season saw vast improvements with double track installed between Derby Castle and Groudle. The double track was also extended to Laxey, making a total route mileage of around seven miles. 1898 saw the next development with the line passing over the impressive Rencell Bridge to gain access to the current location of Laxey Station, allowing an interchange station to be built with the Snaefell Mountain Railway. During this year the line was once again extended, to Ballure (17.25 miles), a temporary terminus on the outskirts of Ramsey. The line from Laxey to Ramsey was financed by a separate company. Trolley collection came into use in 1898, which saw the last use of Hopkinson Bow collectors. Ramsey was finally reached in 1899, completing the full 17.88 mile route we know today. The separate undertaking was financed through Dumbell's bank and the IOMPT&EPC manager Alexander Bruce was found to have used "creative accounting". In 1900, the loans were called in and the bank went bust, with disastrous consequences for the island and the railway. A Manchester based consortium quickly purchased the railway for £252,000 then sold it on for £370,000 to the newly formed Manx Electric Railway Company, which was set up in 1902. The inflated

RAMSEY
- Ballure
- Belle Vue
- Lewaigue
- Dreemskerry
- Ballajora
- Rome's Crossing
- Ballafayle (Corteens)
- Ballaskeig
- Murray's Road / Crowcreen
- Cornaa
- Ballaglass Glen
- Ballagorry
- Glen Mona
- Ballasholague
- Ballig
- Ballellin
- Dhoon Quarry
- Dhoon Glen
- Ballaragh
- Minorca
- Dumbell's Row/ Mines Rd

Note: At the start of the 2015 operating season a number of stops, including Walpole Drive, were removed while new ones such as Derby Castle Car Sheds were added. These remain the same in 2016.

LAXEY STATION
- Laxey Car Shed
- South Cape
- Fairy Cottage
- Ballabeg
- Ballagawne
- Baldrine
- Ballameanagh
- Scarffe's Crossing
- Halfway House
- Eskadale
- Groudle Glen
- Groudle Old Road/Village
- Howstrake
- Far End
- Braeside
- Majestic
- Onchan Head
- Port Jack
- Derby Castle Car Sheds

DOUGLAS DERBY CASTLE

price paid for the railway forced high repayments which led to a lack of investment in the rolling stock and the line for the majority of its ownership. The railway carried on little changed until it was nationalised and taken into Government ownership in 1956/7. A controversial green livery was applied to mark the change. 30th September 1975 saw the closure of the line from Laxey to Ramsey, due to high repair costs and light patronage. However as a knock-on effect, the overall drop in passenger numbers in the operational Douglas-Laxey section was greater than expected and the full line re-opened on 20th June 1977. In 2008, following years of under-investment, the Ramsey line only operated for 58 days on a single track with loop arrangement. The railway has since seen huge investment in the line, infrastructure and trams, which has put it in its safest condition for decades.

1899 built Winter Saloon 21 and 1930 built trailer 40 are seen in the new stopping place for southbound trams in Laxey Station on 5th June 2015. The new paving and crossing has necessitated a new departure stop, the trams previously waiting just behind the photographer, offering new photographic opportunities such as this in the delightful setting that is Laxey Station. **David Umpleby**

Routes and Services

The majority of services start and finish at Douglas and run to Ramsey. During certain timetables odd journeys start and finish at Laxey. With the car shed now closed at Ramsey, it is impossible to stable cars there overnight. Until the mid-2000s the service operated all year round but is now seasonal only, usually starting before Easter and finishing in early November. In years gone by the railway provided a basic timetabled service during the summer and supplemented it with specials and short workings as required. This has now been abolished and all journeys are timetabled. Specials occasionally run for private hires, enthusiasts events and for example, if a cruise ship is visiting the island.

Timetable

Similar to Blackpool, the MER has many peaks and troughs when it comes to passenger loadings and a preserved-railway style series of letter and colour coded timetables operates. This can be anything from just eight journeys on the low-season timetable A, right through to timetable F which offers a 30 minute all day service, plus an evening service, during the busy TT Race period in June. Overall, the earliest a tram ever runs is 08.40 from Douglas. This journey was introduced following the closure of Ramsey depot and runs to provide a 10.10 Ramsey to Douglas. The last journey of a normal day timetable is 17.40 from Ramsey, but timetables F and G include a very late 22.25 from Ramsey, due Douglas 23.40. This new late journey will run for the first time in 2016 and is the latest tram on the railway for decades. A further new initiative for 2016 is the advertised allocation of either car 1 or 2 to work the 13.40 Douglas - Ramsey, 15.10 return on timetable D. With the service usually maintained by enclosed saloons and open trailers, this will be the first time that passengers have the opportunity to ride on the 'oldest tram car in the world', on a regular, scheduled and pre-advertised basis. Details of which timetable runs on which day are beyond the scope of this publication but can be viewed and downloaded from a well designed and nicely colour coded document on the IOM government website.

Fares and Tickets

Go Cards are in use for bus and rail journeys with Isle of Man Transport, as well as traditional cash payments on single journeys and 1 Day Go Explore tickets. Single and return tickets are available from the conductor, ranging from £4.40 for an adult, although this is for a very short journey and Go Explore tickets offer the best value. An adult return from Derby Castle to Ramsey (the full extent of the line) is £12.40 and £6.20 for a child.

	Adult	Child	Family
1 Day Go Explore	£16.00	£8.00	£39.00
3 Day Go Explore	£32.00	£16.00	£75.00
5 Day Go Explore	£39.00	£19.50	£95.00
7 Day Go Explore	£47.00	£23.50	£115.00

Go Explore cards can be purchased at Derby Castle, Laxey or Ramsey on the MER, the Welcome Centre at the Sea Terminal and Ronaldsway Airport information desk.

There is also a whole range of tickets for local residents.

These prices are based on the 2015 price structure and are subject to change.

Key Location

Laxey has always been an important and busy location. Many MER passengers alight here and transfer to the Snaefell Mountain Railway. The two systems can be viewed side by side. The MER car sheds at Laxey are used as an overnight stabling point for car sets, which can be seen propelling into the station before the first morning service car, and back out in the evening.

The Fleet

The fleet is split into operational and withdrawn stock. The 2015 operational fleet comprised 13 motors and 13 trailers, plus 11 motors and 10 trailers considered as withdrawn and stored. All of the original rolling stock was delivered between 1893 and 1906 and is of distinctly American influence, featuring enclosed saloon and open sided Toastrack motor cars and trailers, reflecting the interurban nature of the line. Cars 1 and 2 are appropriately recorded as the oldest electric trams in the world still in use on their original line. At its peak, the fleet consisted of 32 passenger motor cars and 29 trailers, many of which survive today. Eleven

Cornaa is the tranquil setting for this photo of 22+51. Trailer 51 is the oldest operating trailer on the MER, dating back to the dawn of the line in 1893, when it would have just operated to Groudle. The sight of the small lightweight trailers north of Laxey is very rare indeed, especially behind one of the heavy Winter Saloons. The white fence on the left of the photo has a new sign for Cornaa International, believed to have been put up by a local enthusiast! **David Umpleby**

The Manx Electric Railway holds annual enthusiast events based around the Island's railways and are a must for any tram or rail enthusiast. As part of the opening for the 2015 events the line's two original power cars were run in parallel from Derby Castle to Groudle and return. The pair are seen here climbing back to Howstrake in glorious summer sun. Car 1 carries the wording of the original cars. Although the livery is incorrect for this wording, it adds a historic feel.
David Umpleby

vehicles were lost in the Laxey Depot fire in 1930 including motor cars 3, 4, 8 and 24. Three trailers were supplied new by English Electric in Preston to make good the loss. Three of the vestibuled saloons of 1895 were withdrawn during 1902-4, rebuilt for freight use then scrapped in the 1920s; only one member of the class survives today as Freight car 26. Many of the Toastracks which survive today are no longer in use, with some having lain idle since the 1970s. More recently, saloon car 22 was destroyed by fire in 1992 and reconstructed to largely original specification. During 1995 the Snaefell Mountain Railway celebrated its centenary. As part of the celebrations a replica works car based on SMR No.7 'Maria' was built and saw limited use on the mountain. Afterwards the body was taken to the MER, mounted on 3ft gauge trucks and used as a works car on and off for several years, however it was last used in February 2015 and is currently withdrawn. Tunnel Car 7 had to be rebuilt in 2010 after many years of neglect, and is also considered to be new or rebuilt. It carries an approximation of the livery it would have had when new - blue with white and teak - giving it a very striking and smart appearance. Trailer 48 was painted to match and these tend to run as a pair. Open Toastrack 14, known as a 'Ratchet' due to its reliance on its handbrake, had been stored since 1982 but is currently under overhaul and should return to service shortly in original 1898 livery. A few historic mail vans and freight wagons are also operational.

Ramsey Station has been living on borrowed time for the last few years, with plans in place for a new interchange station to incorporate bus and tram operations in one central location for the first time. Therefore the usual shot at Ramsey will be confined to the archives. On 7th June 2015 time seems to have stood still on the MER with Cars 32+57 and Cars 2+43 sharing the northern terminus. The sight of one of these cars at Ramsey is considered rare: both there at the same time is exceedingly rare! Cars 1 and 2 are advertised to run on service in 2016, on a designated journey in the summer timetable, a new initiative, designed to increase patronage. A welcome addition! **David Umpleby**

The Future

The railway is still receiving the much needed investment which has been missing throughout its history. In 2014/15 it won the 'Project of the Year under 50m Euro' at the Light Rail Awards, following the refurbishment of 1898-built Ballure bridge. Alongside this has been constant track renewal and the installation of new substation electrical equipment. The railway is a tourist attraction and as such will not see any changes in terms of extensions or cut-backs in the foreseeable future. Although with the future of the Douglas Horse Tramway remaining uncertain, if it is relaid, there remains the possibility of the MER finally extending to the Sea Terminal at Douglas.

Fleet details:
24 4-axle bogie single deck motor cars built 1893-1906/1992
Seats: Various
Equipment: Various

No.	Built	Built by	Type	Notes
1	1893	G. F. Milnes	Unvestibuled Saloon	
2	1893	G. F. Milnes	Unvestibuled Saloon	
5	1894	G. F. Milnes	Saloon	
6	1894	G. F. Milnes	Saloon	
7	1894	G. F. Milnes	Saloon	Heavily rebuilt between 2007 and 2010
9	1894	G. F. Milnes	Saloon	Fitted with illuminations
14	1898	G. F. Milnes	Crossbench	Under restoration
15	1898	G. F. Milnes	Crossbench	Stored
16	1898	G. F. Milnes	Crossbench	
17	1898	G. F. Milnes	Crossbench	Stored
18	1898	G. F. Milnes	Crossbench	Stored
19	1899	G. F. Milnes	Saloon	
20	1899	G. F. Milnes	Saloon	
21	1899	G. F. Milnes	Saloon	
22	1992	McArd Contractors Ltd	Saloon	
25	1898	G. F. Milnes	Crossbench	Stored
26	1898	G. F. Milnes	Crossbench	Stored
27	1898	G. F. Milnes	Crossbench	Stored
28	1904	ER&TCC	Crossbench	Stored
29	1904	ER&TCC	Crossbench	Stored
30	1904	ER&TCC	Crossbench	Stored
31	1904	ER&TCC	Crossbench	Stored
32	1906	UEC	Crossbench	
33	1906	UEC	Crossbench	

Fleet details:
23 4-axle bogie single deck trailer cars built 1893-1906/1930
Seats: Various
Equipment: None

No.	Built	Built by	Type	Notes
36	1894	G. F. Milnes	Crossbench	Stored
37	1894	G. F. Milnes	Crossbench	Stored
40	1930	English Electric	Crossbench	
41	1930	English Electric	Crossbench	
42	1903	G. F. Milnes	Crossbench	Stored
43	1903	G. F. Milnes	Crossbench	
44	1930	English Electric	Crossbench	
46	1899	G. F. Milnes	Crossbench	
47	1899	G. F. Milnes	Crossbench	
48	1899	G. F. Milnes	Crossbench	
49	1893	G. F. Milnes	Crossbench	Stored
50	1893	G. F. Milnes	Crossbench	Stored
51	1893	G. F. Milnes	Crossbench	
53	1893	G. F. Milnes	Crossbench	Stored
54	1893	G. F. Milnes	Crossbench	Stored
55	1904	ER&TCC	Crossbench	Stored
56	1995	ER&TCC	Saloon*	[A]
57	1904	ER&TCC	Unvestibuled Saloon	
58	1904	ER&TCC	Unvestibuled Saloon	Under repair
59	1895	G. F. Milnes	Unvestibuled Saloon	Stored
60	1896	G. F. Milnes	Crossbench	
61	1906	UEC	Crossbench	Stored
62	1906	UEC	Crossbench	Stored

Notes:
[A] This tram was originally a Crossbench trailer (built 1904) but was converted in 1994/95 to a Saloon Trailer with a dedicated area to convey passengers in wheelchairs. It was fitted with a mechanical lift for loading/unloading.

Works Cars:

No.	Built	Built by	Type	Notes
34	1995	MER	Works car	Stored
45	1899	G. F. Milnes	Bogie Flat	(ex-passenger trailer)
52	1893	G. F. Milnes	Bogie Flat with scissor lift	(ex-passenger trailer)

Over the winter of 2014/15 the impressive bridge over Ballure was rebuilt and updated. This has been recognised by several awards showing the exceptional level of work lavished on this structure. Winter Saloon 22 and Trailer 46 are seen heading south out of Ramsey on 10th June 2015. This is the kind of weather in which the open trailer cars are perfect to enjoy the magnificent views the Island has to offer. Winter Saloon 22 is the only Winter Saloon to carry the old MER crests on its body side. **David Umpleby**

Snaefell Mountain Railway
Isle of Man

Vital Statistics

Opened: 1895
Operated by: Isle of Man Government (Isle of Man Railways)
Number of lines: One
Depot: Laxey
Route mileage: 4.9 (7.8 km)
Track gauge: 3ft 6in (1067mm)
Line voltage: 550V DC overhead line
Website: www.gov.im/publictransport

Background

The Snaefell Mountain Railway opened in 1895 at a cost of £40,000, connecting Laxey village with the summit of the Island's largest peak and only mountain Snaefell, 4.9 miles away and 2,036 feet above sea level. Incredibly the line only took eight months to build. The chief promoters of the line had a vested interest in other businesses on the island, including the Manx Electric Railway which afforded the connection (albeit via a short walk from the SMR car shed to the Laxey MER station) to the island's capital, Douglas. The line was designed as a stand-alone railway, and adopted a wider track gauge (3 feet 6 inches) than the MER's 3 feet gauge. The wider spacing of the mountain line's rails allowed for the installation of the central "Fell" incline rail, onto which Fell's patented braking system would act. This was a necessary requirement due to the severe gradients experienced, which average 1 in 12. The Fell rail is now only used in an emergency, as the rheostatic brake is adequate when travelling downhill, with trams climbing conventionally via rail adhesion. Overhead electric current collection was installed, as with the MER, and the mountain trams were equipped with similar large bow collectors to those fitted to the coastal cars. Although the MER switched to trolley arms very early on, the mountain cars have retained the bows, which are less susceptible to the strong winds experienced along the exposed route.

For the opening of the line, six passenger trams numbered 1-6 were supplied by G.F. Milnes in Birkenhead. All were painted in a Prussian blue, white and teak livery, replaced by red, teak and white from 1899, and all six remain in use today albeit that car 5 is basically a replica, constructed in 1971 following a severe fire. A works car also existed, no.7 (and named 'Maria'), which was supplied without bogies and designed to borrow a set from a passenger tram when required for use, often car 5, although others were used. This car fell into disuse and was dumped outside the car shed where it remained for many years until extracted to provide patterns to create a replica for the line's centenary in 1995.

Snaefell Summit was provided with a hotel of basic timber construction to offer refreshments to day visitors. This was replaced in 1906 with a more substantial building which lasted until destroyed by fire in 1982, and this was itself replaced with a new building from 1984.

The railway was sold in 1896 to the Isle of Man Tramways & Electric Power Co., placing it into the same ownership as the Manx Electric Railway, and the following year it was extended a short distance from the original terminus at the car shed to Laxey MER station where an interchange was created. This included a dual gauge siding, shared with the MER, to allow mountain cars to be swapped onto MER trailer bogies for onward transport to the MER's Derby

Castle depot for overhaul. No heavy engineering facilities existed in the SMR depot until rebuilding in 1994/5 finally saw the line able to undertake its own overhauls. Indeed, with engineering now taken in-house, the dual gauge siding was finally removed during a reconstruction of Laxey station during the winter of 2013/14.

The IoMT&EP Co. went into liquidation in 1900 and the railway, along with the MER, was sold to the Manx Electric Railway Co. Ltd. in 1902. The two World Wars saw the railway cease operation, as tourism on a remote island was nonexistent. It was closed from 9th August 1914 to 9th June 1919 and 20th September 1939 to 1st June 1946.

After over 50 years operation by the MER Co., financial difficulties forced nationalisation of both the SMR and the MER in 1957, and a new green livery was applied to a couple of members of the fleet. However, as with the MER, the earlier livery was soon reinstated following complaints, and the line continued to look much as it did in its formative years.

For the majority of their lives the Snaefell cars have remained largely unchanged. However the two most obviously different cars are seen in this view from 4th June 2015 in Laxey station. The new paving installed here over the winter of 2014/15 changes the scene forever. Car 5 is a rebuild following a fire which destroyed the original car 5 at the Summit in 1970, the 'new' car being built in 1971 and is easy to recognise as it has no clerestory roof. Car 1 received the most major overhaul to date and entered service in 2013 in the original livery of Prussian blue and ivory and looks very striking. **David Umpleby**

One significant change befell car 5, which caught fire at the summit in 1970 following an underfloor short circuit and was (with the exception of one cab end) destroyed above the underframe. The fire was believed to have been caused by the constant swapping of bogies with no.7. The underframe and bogies were refurbished and local woodworking specialists H.D. Kinnin of Ramsey were contracted to supply a replica body. This omitted the clerestory roof and featured bus style saloon windows, giving car 5 a different if unwanted look. More authentic wooden framed windows were restored to car 5 during a further rebuild in 2003.

The 1970s saw a period of change for the SMR, with the re-equipping of the tram fleet with more modern equipment salvaged from withdrawn trams from Aachen in Germany. The project, undertaken jointly with London Transport, saw seven Aachen cars purchased for parts, and six of these moved to LT's Acton works where the motors were fitted into new bogies which incorporated the original Snaefell wheelsets and Fell gear. The Aachen controllers and resistors (the latter now roof mounted) were fitted to the Snaefell cars at the MER's Derby Castle depot. The final Aachen car actually made it to the Isle of Man, full of spares, and was dumped outside Derby Castle depot where it remained for several years until eventually being scrapped.

A very traditional looking scene at the Summit of the Snaefell Mountain Railway with Car 4. This tram is currently undergoing an overhaul. Shortly before withdrawal from traffic in 2015, car 4 was fitted with exterior illuminations as part of the 120th anniversary celebrations. Unfortunately the day's events were somewhat muted by the poor weather, just going to show you can never beat the weather on the Mountain!
David Umpleby

Infrastructure improvements saw a new depot and workshops provided at Laxey in 1994/5, ahead of the centenary of the line in 1995, whilst a replica of the original works car was constructed as an added centenary attraction. This saw little use and has since transferred to the MER where, renumbered 34, it has become a diesel works car. Major track replacement has taken place in recent years, and during winter 2013/14 this has included a new layout at Laxey station.

The line has always been a seasonal operation as there is very little demand for transport to the summit during the cold winter months. Indeed, to protect the infrastructure from frost damage (and theft) the overhead line is taken down each winter on the most exposed upper sections of the line. However, access to a radar station at the summit, maintained by the Civil Aviation Authority, is required all year round and this is maintained during the winter by use of a Wickham personnel carrier, housed at Laxey in a building adjacent to the running shed.

Services have continued now for almost 120 years, and to honour this achievement pioneer car 1 was outshopped, following overhaul, in 2013 in an assumed version of the original blue, white and teak livery, not seen on the line since 1899. Car 1 now provides an attractive addition to the fleet and a contrast with the more usual red, teak and white cars on the line.

Routes and Services

Services have always run to a similar pattern since inception. Although the pattern is seasonal (mid-March to early-November), the railway operates to a colour coded timetable in a similar style to the Manx Electric Railway. In previous years it just ran to demand with no set timetable. Services are simply Laxey to Summit. The busiest time is during the TT bike races, during which the railway is split into two halves. Services run from Laxey to Bungalow and from Bungalow to Summit, with passengers using a footbridge over the A18 Mountain Road. This normally involves four trams on the lower section and two trams on the upper section, operating on separate tracks.

Timetables

The first passenger journey of the day normally connects with the arrival of the first tram from Douglas, departing five minutes later. This is 10.15 for most of the year. After this trams are usually every 30 minutes with the last departure at 15.45. They normally have a 25 minute layover at the summit, with the last one back at 16.40. Journey time is 30 minutes. Late evening journeys never operated historically, although this has changed following the introduction of the sunset dinners served at the Summit cafe. On a number of dates in 2016, there are 18.25 and 19.25 departures from Laxey, 20.50 and 21.50 back, which connect at Laxey for late trams to Douglas (and, on the 20.50, to Ramsey). When the sunset dinners began, non-dining passengers were able to travel on the trams (using their Explorer passes or buying an ordinary return) but this has now ceased - making them exclusively for diners! If you want to travel up the mountain in the evening you have to pay the full dining fare, even if you don't want to dine!

Fares and Tickets

Go Cards are in use for bus and rail journeys with Isle of Man Transport, as well as traditional cash payments on single journeys and 1 Day Go Explore tickets.

	Adult	Child	Family
1 Day Go Explore	£16.00	£8.00	£39.00
3 Day Go Explore	£32.00	£16.00	£75.00
5 Day Go Explore	£39.00	£19.50	£95.00
7 Day Go Explore	£47.00	£23.50	£115.00

Go Explore cards can be purchased at Derby Castle, Laxey or Ramsey on the MER, the Welcome Centre at the Sea Terminal and Ronaldsway Airport information desk.

Single and return tickets can still be purchased, with a return fare on the MER for an adult from Douglas to Snaefell priced at £14.00.

These prices are based on the 2015 price structure and are subject to change.

Key Location

Given the fact the SMR climbs a mountain, there are a limited number of lineside photographic locations. Laxey station, where all services start and finish, is probably the best location to see the trams. Alternatively, alight at Bungalow where it's possible to appreciate the gradients and take zoom and landscape shots.

Fleet details:
6 bogie saloon cars built in 1895 by G.F. Milnes, Birkenhead
Seats: 48
Equipment: Kiepe 4 x 50kw motors

No.	Built	Notes
1	1895	Heavily rebuilt between 2010 and 2013
2	1895	
3	1895	
4	1895	Overhaul in progress
5	1895 (1971)	Largely destroyed by fire, 1970. Rebuilt by H.D. Kinnin (Ramsey), 1971
6	1895	

Douglas Bay Horse Tramway
Isle of Man

Vital Statistics

Opened: 1876
Operator: Douglas Borough Council
Number of lines: One
Car depot: Strathallan Crescent (Derby Castle)
Horse stables: Summer Hill Road
Route mileage: 1.6 (2.6km)
Track gauge: 3ft (914mm)
Website: www.douglas.gov.im

Victoria Pier ⚪

Gaiety Theatre ⚪

Broadway ⚪

Palace Hotel Casino ⚪

Hydro Hotel ⚪

Strathallan Crescent ⚪
(Stables)

Derby Castle ⚪

The Douglas Horse Tramway is the oldest surviving tramway in the British Isles, and the only remaining UK tramway to still use horses for propulsion. First opened in August 1876, its promoter was Thomas Lightfoot, a retired civil engineer from Sheffield. Due to financial restraints and sporadic operating conditions, initially the line was a single track affair with several passing loops, which made it very slow and unreliable. 1882 saw a change of ownership to the Isle of Man Tramways & Electric Power Co., later the builders of the electric railway to Groudle in 1893. Several extensions saw the tramway reach its most northerly extent in 1890 when it reached Derby Castle - three years before the Manx Electric Railway opened!

In 1894 the tramway changed hands again, following acquisition by the Douglas & Laxey Coast Electric Tramway Ltd. (later the Isle of Man Tramways & Electric Power Co.), which was in the process of opening the coastal tramway between Douglas and Laxey. Improvements at Derby Castle saw an interchange station provided between the two lines, whilst route improvements including track doubling were set to pave the way for a possible extension of Manx Electric Railway services over the horse tramway towards central Douglas. Despite gaining Council approval, this aspiration proved too much for local residents who were concerned by the plan for overhead electric wires along Douglas Promenade, so the dream of electric trams running towards the town centre remained unfulfilled. This was even depicted in postcards of the time which showed horse trams with the horses removed and trolley poles painted on top of the cars! Two years later and a new larger, purpose built car depot was built at the northern end of the tramway at Derby Castle. An attempt to finance the company in February 1900 failed and the I.O.T. & E.P. went into liquidation. The system once again changed hands in September 1901 with Douglas Corporation paying £50,000 for both the horse tramway and the Upper Douglas cable tramway. This had a lasting impact on its future, as its position as a separately run undertaking changed its fortunes in the modern era.

The new owners completed the doubling of the system, a process achieved in part previously, and were again approached by the MER board with a view to taking over and electrifying the line as an MER extension. This idea was, once again, rejected, with the idea firmly laid to rest by 1908. The winter service was stopped as early as 1927, the introduction of cheaper and more comfortable (especially in winter) motor buses seeing off the patronage.

Despite the withdrawal of the winter service and the all conquering motor buses taking hold, there was still significant investment during the 1930s. This saw the track completely relaid, although it took some twenty years to complete! The need to operate during the profitable summer months obviously had to take precedent. Along with the track, there was investment in the rolling stock and new offices were built over the existing car depot at Derby Castle.

The Second World War saw a dramatic change in the tramway's fortunes and which could easily have seen its demise, as was the case on the nearby Douglas Head Marine Drive Electric Tramway which closed for the War and never re-opened. The horse tramway stopped running from September 1939 till May 1946, with the horses sold off.

1949 saw the eight remaining double deck trams sold off, along with the surviving short toastracks in an attempt to reduce the scale of operation. By this time the uniqueness of the horse tramway was starting to be realised and celebrations were held in 1956 to commemorate 80 years of service.

Despite changing fashions, the horse tramway continued to operate each summer season. It celebrated its centenary in 1976 with the return to the line of the last surviving double deck car, a former South Shields tram which had operated in Douglas from 1887 until withdrawal in 1949 and had been on static display at the museum of transport in Clapham. Car 14 is now in the Manx Museum.

Following the celebrations of 1976, patronage continued to decline significantly leading to financial losses and frequent calls for abandonment. The operating season continued to be shortened and the tram fleet was reduced in size as certain examples have departed for preservation or other uses, and indeed many of the retained trams only see very occasional use.

Car 36 built by G.F.Milnes in 1896 seen outside the Strathallan depot. The depot traverser can be seen next to the tram, denoting that the tram had been pulled out for display purposes, as it can't actually get out otherwise! Car 36 with its enclosed roof and bulkheads is one of the more heavily used cars. **David Umpleby**

During the following years, the tramway has suffered from severe under-investment, with the track falling into a deplorable state. Although the track is in grooved rail, the trams often run on their flanges in the bottom of the groove as the track is so excessively worn. All intermediate points have had their blades removed, although the track in between is still in place. The trams themselves have been under-maintained for a number of years, the need for only two serviceable trams meaning that maintenance is not a priority.

Plans for the reconstruction of the promenade in both 2015 and 2016 would have seen the horse tramway operating for the last time in its traditional surroundings in 2014 and then 2015. However its operators have seemingly been unable to agree with Isle of Man Government as to the best position and operation of the tramway, which lead to a temporary reprieve in 2015, but not 2016 (see below).

It is a unique survivor.

A line up of open crossbench horse cars 43, 36 and saloon 27 at Strathallan Crescent. **Nick Meskell**

Routes and Services

While this book was in production it was announced that the Horse Tramway would not be operating in 2016. Numerous reasons were cited including the further delay in promenade reconstruction, the cost of operating the service and the loss it makes plus other issues involving Manx politics. Although the MER, IMR and SMR all come under the umbrella of the Manx Government and are funded accordingly, the Horse Trams are run by Douglas Corporation, which is funded differently, despite also being under the Manx Government! As this book went to press there were a number of options on the table: close altogether; operate a partial service; find the money and operate a full service; let Isle of Man Transport run the service, plus a few others. Before visiting this tramway please consult the Manx press (such as www.iomtoday.co.im) and the OFFICIAL websites. Beware of unofficial/out of date sites.

Timetables

During recent years, the service has been seasonal only, usually from May until September. A two car service was the normal operation, offering a basic 20 minute frequency. The journey took approximately 20 minutes. The first tram from Derby Castle was at 09.00 and the last tram from the Sea Terminal was 17.40.

Fares and Tickets

In 2015, single journey tickets were £3.00 for adults, £2.00 for under 16s and free of charge for accompanied children under five. These could be purchased from the conductor on board, at tram stations and online. An all day adult ticket was £5.70. Go Explore cards and Island Explorer tickets were accepted.

Key Location

The key location was probably the Derby Castle terminus. Here it is possible to see all arrivals and departures, cars stabled awaiting service and shunting to and from the depot. Horses are usually changed here. Sandwiched between the MER, the Terminus Tavern and public toilets, and opposite the promenade, beach and sea, when it comes to idyllic locations, it doesn't get much better than this!

Fleet details:
19 2-axle horse drawn cars built 1883-1913 by various manufacturers

No.	Built	Built by	Type	Notes
1	1913	Milnes Voss	Enclosed saloon	
12	1888	G. F. Milnes	Open Toastrack	Returned to service on last day of service in 2014
18	1883	Metropolitan Railway Carriage & Wagon Co.	Double Deck	Ex-South Shields. Oldest operable tram car.
21	1890	G. F. Milnes	Open Toastrack	
27	1892	G. F. Milnes	Enclosed Saloon	
28	1892	G. F. Milnes	Enclosed Saloon	
29	1892	G. F. Milnes	Enclosed Saloon	
32	1896	G. F. Milnes	Crossbench	
33	1896	G. F. Milnes	Crossbench	
34	1896	G. F. Milnes	Crossbench	
36	1896	G. F. Milnes	Crossbench	
37	1896	G. F. Milnes	Crossbench	
38	1902	G. F. Milnes	Open Toastrack	
39	1902	G. F. Milnes	Open Toastrack	
40	1902	G. F. Milnes	Open Toastrack	
42	1905	Milnes Voss	Open Toastrack	Special livery, similar style to 44. Red and blue.
43	1907	United Electric Car Co.	Crossbench	
44	1907	United Electric Car Co.	Crossbench	Special livery, Royal Tram. Red and blue.
45	1908	Milnes Voss	Crossbench	

Volk's Electric Railway
Brighton

Vital Statistics

Opened: 1883
Operator: Brighton & Hove City Council
Depot: Halfway
Route mileage: 1.25 (2.0km)
Power supply: 110V DC third rail
Track gauge: 2ft 8½in (825mm)
Website: www.volkselectricrailway.co.uk

Aquarium Station

Halfway Station

Black Rock Station

Background

The Volk's Electric Railway in Brighton is the oldest operating electric railway in the world; only the Gross-Lichterfelde tramway in Berlin, which opened in 1881 and closed in 1931, had preceded Volk's railway. The line was constructed by Magnus Volk, with the first section opening in August 1883, and it survives in operation to this day as a monument to the experimental technology of the era and as a forerunner to all electrically powered tramways and railways ever built.

Brighton Corporation took control of the line in 1940, later passing to Brighton & Hove Council. The Volk's Electric Railway Society was formed in 1995 to assist the Council with the operation of the line, and the Society has remained active in the operation and promotion of the line since this time.

During the summer of 2014 it was revealed that, following a bid by Brighton & Hove City Council, the VER had been awarded £1,593,800 by the Heritage Lottery Fund to allow for refurbishment and restoration of the line. The money will provide a new visitor centre and ticket office at the Aquarium station, a new depot, vehicle restoration and the development of new learning materials and educational sessions for schools, and will help to ensure that this electric pioneer carries passengers along the sea front for many years to come.

The Route

The railway operates for 1.25 miles along the seafront following Madeira Drive from Brighton Aquarium to Black Rock. The route has varied in length over the years: the original ¼ mile route ran from the Aquarium to the future site of the Palace Pier. It was extended in 1884 to a location called Paston Place (now the Halfway station), adding a further ½ mile of route length, the system being re-gauged to 2ft. 9in. and the voltage increased to 160V at this time. In 1886 the track gauge was reduced to 2ft. 8½in. (825mm), and the current supply moved to an independent third rail providing 110V DC. Following the closure in 1901 of Volk's other electric railway, the curious Brighton and Rottingdean Seashore Electric Railway, which ran along the seabed and resembled a mobile section of seaside pier, the Volk's Electric Railway was extended from Paston Place to Black Rock, replacing some of the route of the closed 'Daddy Longlegs'.

In 1930 the route was cut back at the Brighton end, with the terminus relocated from the Palace Pier to a new site at the Aquarium, then in 1937 a similar length of line was cut from the opposite end due to the construction of a new Lido at Black Rock. A new water pumping station, opened at Black Rock in 1998, forced a further cut back of route by about 100 yards, the railway now sharing a station building with the local water board.

Opening Times

The railway is in operation daily from Easter to September with the first trains at 10.15 (11.15 Monday and Friday), and the last trains at 17.00 (18.00 weekends and Bank Holidays). Check website for details.

Fares

Payable at booking offices: Single and return fares are available to Halfway station or for the full route. Full trip return fares are: £3.70 (adult), £2.80 (senior), £2.20 (child), £9.50 (family).

Key Location

Halfway, adjacent to the depot, provides the focal point of the line.

The Fleet

The composition of the fleet has changed over the years and has at times included second hand stock from the Southend Pier Railway. Today's passenger fleet consists of seven open or semi-open four wheel cars built by the Volk's Electric Railway at Brighton between 1892 and 1926. All are equipped with 1 x 6kw motor from either Siemens or Compagnie Electrique Belgique. Operation can be single or in coupled pairs. Cars 3, 4 and 6 are currently unserviceable but are to be returned to use in the near future due to the involvement of the Volk's Electric Railway Society and thanks to Heritage Lottery Funding secured in 2014.

Fleet details:
7 2-axle single deck cars built 1892-1926 by VER, Brighton
Seating: 40
Equipment: 1 x 6kw motor

No.	Built	Built by	Type	Notes
3	1892	VER Brighton	Semi-Open	Withdrawn. Under rebuild
4	1892	VER Brighton	Semi-Open	Withdrawn. Awaiting rebuild
6	1901	VER Brighton	Semi-Open	Withdrawn. Awaiting repairs
7	1901	VER Brighton	Semi-Open	Operational
8	1901	VER Brighton	Semi-Open	Operational
9	1910	VER Brighton	Open	Operational
10	1926	VER Brighton	Open	Operational

Works loco:

No.	Built	Built by	Type	Notes
Works loco	1988 (acquired by VER 2004)	Alan Keef Ltd	Diesel loco	Operational. Reserved for works duties when electric current is switched off.

Seaton Tramway

Vital Statistics

Opened: 1970
Operator: Modern Electric Tramways Limited
Depot: Riverside
Route mileage: 3 (4.8km)
Power supply: 120V DC overhead line
Track gauge: 2ft 9in (825mm)
Website: www.tram.co.uk

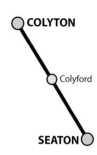

Background

The Seaton Tramway in East Devon operates for three miles between Seaton and Colyton over the route of the former British Railways route from Seaton to Seaton Junction. The tramway was the vision of one man, Claude Lane, and originated in a portable 15in. gauge line which visited funfairs and garden fetes from 1948 until 1950. The first permanent site was at St Leonards-on-Sea in 1951, the tramway then moving to Rhyl the following year.

Operations transferred to Eastbourne from 1955 to provide much needed security of tenure and to allow for expansion. At Eastbourne the track gauge was increased to 2ft and further trams were added to the fleet. However, the desire to own the freehold for the land they occupied led Modern Electric Tramways into negotiations with British Rail regarding the purchase of the former Seaton Junction to Seaton branch, which were concluded in 1969. Services were inaugurated at Seaton in August 1970, operating over about a mile of newly laid track, trams reaching the eventual terminus at Colyton in 1980. A final short extension to a new terminus at Seaton opened in 1995.

No.16, a rebuild of former Bournemouth tram 106, arrives at Seaton terminus with a driver experience charter.
James Millington

*London 'Feltham' styled tram 12 crosses the main road at Colyford with a journey towards Seaton. **James Millington***

The Route

Trams start from a two track terminus at Seaton, beyond which is the previous stub terminus which is still used for stabling spare trams during the day. The section between Seaton and Riverside depot was constructed on a new alignment in 1975 to bring the trams to a prominent location in the town and due to the fact that the former railway track bed from here into the town had been sold for redevelopment. From Riverside depot, trams proceed north on the trackbed of the former Seaton to Seaton Junction branch line, following the River Axe to Colyford. Although the line is mostly single track, passing loops are provided at Riverside, Axmouth, Swan's Nest and Colyford.

The tramway crosses the main A3052 road at Colyford, which requires tram drivers to activate railway style warning signals to stop oncoming road traffic. From here to Colyton, the tramway leaves the River Axe behind but continues to follow the route of the old railway line, with passing loops at Tye Lane and Cownhayne, to the former Colyford Station which has been refurbished to become tea rooms and a shop. Although essentially reserved track throughout the length of the tramway, the short section of double track within the limits of Colyton Station have been paved to give something of the impression of an Edwardian street.

Opening Times

The tramway operates daily from April until the end of October and at limited times during the winter season. Check website for details.

*Leaving Seaton for Colyton, car 8 rounds Poppy Corner on its way along the 1975 extension built to connect the former railway trackbed to the town centre. **James Millington***

Fares

Tickets can be booked online in advance or purchased from booking offices at each end of the line. The All Day Explorer ticket at £10.00 (adult), £6.70 (child) and £30.00 (family) offers the best value for exploring the tramway. Please note these prices increase slightly during the peak season when some evening journeys are provided.

Key Location

The attractive Colyton Station provides something resembling a typical street scene environment for the tramway and is a particularly attractive location. The trolley reverser at the terminus also adds interest to the scene.

Fleet details:
13 4-axle single or double deck cars built (or rebuilt) 1956-1998 by Modern Electric Tramways, Eastbourne and Seaton, or 2002 by Bolton Trams Ltd, Salford
Seating: Various
Equipment: Various

No.	Built	Notes
2	1964	Metropolitan Electric Tramways style bogie double deck
4	1961	Blackpool Open Boat bogie single deck
6	1954	Llandudno & Colwyn Bay style bogie double deck
7*	1958	Llandudno & Colwyn Bay style bogie double deck
8	1968	Llandudno & Colwyn Bay style bogie double deck
9	2002	Plymouth and Blackburn bogie double deck cars
10	2002	Plymouth and Blackburn bogie double deck cars
11	2002	Plymouth and Blackburn bogie double deck cars
12	1966	London Feltham bogie double deck
14	1904/1984	Ex-Metropolitan Electric Tramways no.94
16	1921/1992	Ex-Bournemouth no.106
17	1988	Manx Electric Railway crossbench single deck
19	1906/1998	Ex-Exeter no.19

* Stored unserviceable

Works cars:

No.	Built	Notes
02	1952	Freelance works car

A number of wagons exist for various works purposes, numbered 01, 03-05

Great Orme Tramway
Llandudno

Vital Statistics

Opened: 1902
Operator: Conway County Borough Council
Depot: Victoria Station, Halfway, Summit
Route mileage: 1.25 (2.0km)
Power supply: Cable haulage
Track gauge: 3ft 6in (1067mm)
Website: www.greatormetramway.co.uk

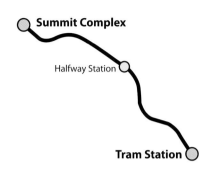

Summit Complex

Halfway Station

Tram Station

Background

The Great Orme Tramway in Llandudno is a cable hauled funicular which has been in operation between Victoria Station and the Great Orme Summit since 1902/3. The system is physically divided into two sections, with the lower portion between Victoria and Halfway stations operating on (or alongside) the public highway, whilst the upper portion from Halfway to just below the Summit is wholly on a reserved track alignment. The tramway is not a cable-car system whereby the trams grip a continuously moving cable, as required for propulsion (like in San Francisco), but a funicular with the trams physically attached to the cable and controlled by a winding house acting on the instructions of the driver. The upper section is also a counterbalance system, with the two cars connected together; the one going downhill helping to pull the other one up.

The tramway was sold to the Great Orme Railway Ltd in 1934. In 1940 Llandudno UDC sought to exercise powers granted in 1898 to take ownership, but due to the outbreak of war

*The other lower section car, no 4, is seen climbing towards its next stop at the aptly named Halfway Station as car 5 descends in the background. The views from this well-kept survivor are second to none on a clear day. **Nick Meskell***

(throughout which the line carried on as normal) this was deferred until 1949. After many years operating as the 'Great Orme Railway', the title 'Great Orme Tramway' was reinstated from 1977.

Ownership was transferred to Conway County Council in 1996, but in 2000 it was closed following separate incidents on both sections of the tramway. As a result, a new state of the art communication system was installed, allowing re-opening the following year. Investment has continued with a comprehensive overhaul of all four trams and a new station building provided at Halfway from 2001.

Car 5 is seen on a sunny but cold morning negotiating the tight curve on the Ty-Gwyn Road section. The severity of the gradient can be seen here. **Nick Meskell**

The Route

The tramway is divided into two separate and unconnected sections. The lower part begins at Victoria Station on Church Walks and ends at Halfway Station. It resembles a traditional tramway operating either on, or alongside, the public highway. The single track line departs uphill along the narrow and steeply graded Old Road, before turning slightly left to run alongside Ty-Gwyn Road, where the passing loop for this section is situated. From here to the station at Halfway the track is interlaced and continues on a steep grade alongside Ty-Gwyn Road to Halfway.

The upper section features open reserved track throughout. Departing from Halfway Station on a level grade, the single track line crosses St Tudno's Road and continues towards the passing loop for this section. On exiting the passing loop the single track line then climbs through an embankment to reach Summit station.

Opening Times

The tramway is in operation daily from late March to late October, with trams running every 20 minutes from 10.00 until 18.00 (17.00 March and October).

Fares

Payable at booking offices. Return fares: £6.50 (adult), £4.50 (child).

Key Location

The tramway can be captured against the spectacular backdrop of Llandudno Bay on Ty-Gwyn Road, close to its junction with Ty'-n-Y-Coed Road. This is on the lower section between the midway passing loop and Halfway Station.

The Fleet

The tramway is still operated by the original rolling stock which consists of four bogie single deck trams built by Hurst Nelson & Co. of Motherwell in 1902/3. Two cars (4 and 5) work the lower section, with the other two (6 and 7) permanently resident on the upper portion. All were supplied with mechanical wheel and track brakes, whilst the lower section pair also featured a powerful spring brake which would deploy into the cable conduit channel if a loss of tension was detected. This latter brake was disconnected without replacement in 1906 after causing too many delays due to spurious activations, which left the cars without an emergency braking system. This issue was finally rectified in 1934 following the design of a new automatic brake which monitored the trams and would deploy if speed increased to greater than 2mph beyond the speed of the cable, which moved at a maximum of 4mph.

For the 1991 season the lower section cars gained an ornate livery style, which was applied to the upper section cars the following year. The repaints coincided with all four cars receiving names for the very first time, the names being those associated with local North Wales saints, but which had also appeared on ships operating between Liverpool and North Wales.

Fleet details:
4 4-axle bogie single deck cars built 1902-1903 by Hurst Nelson & Co., Motherwell
Seating: 48
Equipment: Cable hauled

No.	Name	Built	Built by	Type	Notes
4	St. Tudno	1902	Hurst Nelson	Bogie single deck	Lower section
5	St. Silio	1902	Hurst Nelson	Bogie single deck	Lower section
6	St. Seiriol	1903	Hurst Nelson	Bogie single deck	Upper section
7	St. Trillo	1903	Hurst Nelson	Bogie single deck	Upper section

Museums

National Tramway Museum
Crich

Vital Statistics

Established: 1959
Operated by: The Tramway Museum Society
Route mileage: approximately 1 (1.6km)
Power supply: 550V DC overhead line
Gauge: 4ft 8½in (1435mm)
Address: Crich Tramway Village, Matlock, DE4 5DP
Website: www.tramway.co.uk

Background

The National Tramway Museum is the operating arm of the Tramway Museum Society and has for several years promoted itself as 'Crich Tramway Village'. The museum was established on the site of George Stephenson's mineral railway at Crich in 1959, following the formation of the Society in 1955. The first public services over a short length of line from what had become known as Town End to a point close to the depots were provided by horse cars in 1963; electric traction was inaugurated the following year. Extensions to the line occurred in 1966, bringing the length to approximately 400 yards, and then again in 1968 with a more significant extension to a point known as Wakebridge. Finally, in 1978, the tramway reached its maximum length of approximately one mile when it was extended beyond Wakebridge along a plateau, giving remarkable views of the Amber Valley, to the current terminus at Glory Mine.

The depot complex has been progressively extended to house the expanding fleet, which has grown over the years to be by far the largest collection in the UK. Pressures on space were relieved by the building of a brand new exhibition hall in 1991, whilst other recent projects have seen the workshops extended and a viewing gallery provided, in 2002. The exhibition hall was revamped for 2010, and in 2011 the original Stephenson Workshop was re-opened following restoration. This features an education suite and upper floor exhibition, linked to the workshop gallery via a new walkway.

During the celebrations to commemorate 50 years of electric operation at Crich, held in October 2014, newly restored London United 159 is followed along the museum street by Newcastle 114, visiting from Beamish.
James Millington

Glasgow 'Standard' 812 heads towards Town End at the bandstand/museum entrance stop, with Leeds 180 and Blackpool 166 behind. **James Millington**

The Route

The line begins at Town End and consists of a double track tramway for the first part of its length through Stephenson Place and along the museum's recreated main street. The extensive depot complex on the left hand side also features the workshop and Grand Exhibition Hall. Beyond the depot, the tramway narrows to a short section of interlaced track beneath the Bowes-Lyon bridge, before opening up to double track again by the bandstand. Becoming reserved sleeper track beyond this point, double track ends prior to Cabin Crossing, and token working is in place on the single line section to the halfway passing point at Wakebridge. From here to the terminus at Glory Mine, the tramway is single track again and protected by token working. Glory Mine terminus features a passing loop and reversing stub.

*Above left: The terminus of the tramway at Glory Mine, with Leeds 'Convert' 345 reversing. **James Millington***

*Above right: The access tram, Berlin 223 006-4, and Blackpool 'Brush Railcoach' 630 stand together outside the museum's workshops. **James Millington***

Opening Times

The museum is open daily from late March to early November, check website for details.

Admission Prices

Adult: £16.00
Senior: £12.00
Child: £9.00
Family (2 adults and up to 3 children): £39.00

All admission tickets are valid for a full year from the date of issue

Key Location

The museum's main street, framed at one end by the ornate Bowes-Lyon bridge, acts as the focal point of the tramway. A small number of recreated buildings, including the Red Lion pub from Stoke on Trent, complement original stone buildings surviving from the days of George Stephenson, and combine to add an attractive backdrop to this double track section of the tramway.

Fleet details:

No.	Origin	Built	Status
1	Derby	1904	Static display
1	Douglas Head Marine Drive	1896	Static display
1	Glasgow (works car)	1905	Stored (Clay Cross)
1	Leamington & Warwick	1881	Static display
1	London Transport	1932	Undergoing restoration
2	Blackpool & Fleetwood	1898	Static display
2	Blackpool (railgrinder)	1935	Stored (Clay Cross)
2	Leeds (tower car)	1932	Static display
4	Blackpool Electric Tramway Co.	1885	Static display
5	Blackpool	1972	Stored (Clay Cross)
5	Gateshead & District	1927	Static display
7	Chesterfield	1904	Operational
8	Chesterfield	1904	Static display
9	Oporto	1873	Static display
10	Hill of Howth	1902	Static display
14	Grimsby & Immingham	1915	Static display
15	Sheffield	1874	Operational
21	Cardiff	1886	Static display
21	Dundee & District	1894	Static display
21	Glasgow (stores van)	1903	Stored (Clay Cross)
22	Glasgow	1922	Operational
35	Edinburgh	1948	Static display
39	North Metropolitan Tramways Co.	unk	Static display (one side as a display case in exhibition hall)
40	Blackpool & Fleetwood	1914	Operational, on loan to Blackpool Transport
40	Blackpool	1926	Operational
45	Southampton	1903	Static display
46	Sheffield	1899	Stored (Clay Cross)
47	New South Wales Govt.	1885	Static display
49	Blackpool	1926	Static display
59	Blackpool	1902	Stored (Clay Cross)
60	Johannesburg	1905	Static display
74	Sheffield	1900	Operational
76	Leicester	1904	Static display
84	MBRO	1886	Stored (in parts). (Clay Cross)
102	Newcastle	1901	Static display
106	London County Council	1903	Operational
107	Leeds	1898	Static display
131	Cardiff (water car)	1905	Operational
132	Kingston-upon-Hull	1910	Static display. On loan to Hull Streetlife Museum
159	London United Tramways	1901	Operational
166	Blackpool	1927	Operational
166	Nottingham	1920	Stored (Clay Cross)

Fleet details:

No.	Origin	Built	Status
167	Blackpool	1928	Operational
180	Leeds	1931	Operational
180	Prague	1908	Static display
184	North Metropolitan (horse car body)	c1895	Stored (in parts)
189	Sheffield	1934	Static display
236	Blackpool	1934	Operational
249	Blackpool	1935	Static display
264	Sheffield	1937	Static display
273	Oporto	1927	Operational
298	Blackpool	1937	Stored (Clay Cross)
330	Sheffield	1919	Operational
331	Metropolitan Electric	1930	Operational
345	Leeds	1921	Operational
399	Leeds	1926	Operational
510	Sheffield	1950	Operational
600	Leeds	1954	Stored (Clay Cross)
602	Leeds	1953	Static display
630	Blackpool	1937	Operational
674	New York 3rd Ave. Transit	1939	Static display
762	Blackpool	1982	Operational
812	Glasgow	1900	Static display
869	Liverpool	1936	Operational
902	Halle	1969	Static display
1068	Glasgow	1919	Operational
1100	Glasgow	1928	Stored (Clay Cross)
1115	Glasgow	1929	Static display
1147	The Hague	1957	Static display
1282	Glasgow	1940	Static display
1297	Glasgow	1948	Static display
1622	London Transport	1912	Operational
223 006-4	Berlin	1969	Operational
Loco (717)	Blackpool (works car)	1927	Operational
TW4	Crich (tower wagon)	2011	Operational
58	Croydon Tramlink (works car)	1978	Operational
61	Croydon Tramlink (flatbed trailer)	1978	Operational

Heaton Park Tramway
Manchester

Vital Statistics

Established: 1980
Operated by: Manchester Transport Museum Society
Route mileage: approximately 0.5 (0.8km)
Power supply: 550V DC overhead line
Gauge: 4ft 8½in (1435mm)
Address: Heaton Park, Manchester, M25 2SW
Website: www.heatonparktramway.org.uk

Background

The Heaton Park tramway is based on a surviving portion of the once extensive Manchester Corporation Tramway system and is the only preserved tramway in the UK. The tracks within the park were originally abandoned in 1934, but following the discovery of the body of a former Manchester Corporation single deck tram during the 1960s, the impetus was provided to uncover the surviving tracks within Heaton Park to provide a short demonstration line on which to operate the tram, once restored. The tracks within the park were reopened in 1980, and a former waiting shelter was converted into a depot and museum, to house the tram. The line has been extended a number of times, and now continues to Lakeside where a second depot was constructed to house the expanding tram fleet.

The Route

From Middleton Road gates the route takes a straight line double track alignment to the museum and depot over the surviving tracks of the former Manchester Corporation system. Beyond here, more recent extensions take trams on a single track route which turns right onto the park drive and then left onto reserved track through woodland towards Whitegate. The reservation continues beside the park drive to Old Lakeside, where the drive is crossed at near right angles. Trams then turn left to terminate at Lakeside, beyond which lies the second and newer of the two depots.

Opening Times

The tramway is in operation every Sunday from mid February until November. Special events are held throughout the year - check website for details.

Fares

Payable to conductor
Adult: £2.00 return, £5.00 multi-ride   **Child:** £1.00 return, £2.50 multi-ride
Family *(2 adults and 2 children)***:** £5.00 return, £12.50 multi-ride

A former Blackpool tram at Heaton Park is 'Brush Railcoach 623', seen at the Lakeside terminus of the line. **James Millington**

Blackpool 'Vanguard' 619 is a replica created in 1987 from the remains of a former one man operated single deck tram. It has been at Heaton Park since 2010 and carries a fictitious Blackpool Corporation style livery. **James Millington**

Key Location

The most activity can be seen at Lakeside terminus where, in normal operation with two trams in use, one waits while the other makes a journey along the line. On event days and with more trams in use, focus turns to Middleton Road depot and museum. Trams can be seen passing on the double track section between here and the park gates.

Fleet details:

No.	Origin	Built	Status
5	Stockport	1901	Undergoing repairs. On loan from Stockport 5 Tramcar Trust
23	Rawtenstall	1912	Stored (in parts). Awaiting restoration
43	Oldham	1902	Stored. Awaiting restoration
96	Hull	1901	Operational
173	Manchester	1901	Static display
619	Blackpool	1987*	Operational
623	Blackpool	1937	Operational
680	Blackpool	1935	Operational. On loan to Blackpool Transport
702	Blackpool	1935	Stored
708	Blackpool	1935	On loan to NEETT, Sunderland
752	Blackpool (Railgrinder)	1920	Stored
765	Manchester	1914	Operational
1007	Manchester Metrolink	1991	Stored. Metrolink Trafford depot
L53	Manchester (horse car)	c.1880	On loan to Bury Transport Museum

Beamish Museum
County Durham

Vital Statistics

Established: 1970
Operated by: Beamish Museum Limited
Route mileage: approximately 1.5 (2.4km)
Power supply: 550V DC overhead line
Gauge: 4ft 8½in (1435mm)
Address: Beamish Museum, Beamish, County Durham, DH9 0RG
Telephone: 0191 370 4000
Website: www.beamish.org.uk

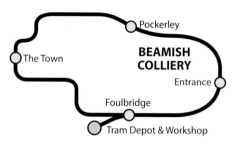

Background

Beamish is the open air 'Living Museum of the North' which is laid out across 300 acres of land previously in private ownership and used for agricultural and mining purposes, and is situated close to the town of Stanley, County Durham. It opened in 1972 with the aim of preserving for future generations a reminder of how life had been for residents of the region during the late Victorian and Edwardian eras, and the replica town takes the visitor instantly back in time to the year 1913. The rural areas of the site are based more closely on the era of the industrial revolution, around 1825.

Standard 147 on its debut running day at Beamish on 5th March 2016. **James Millington**

Newcastle 114 departs from the town towards Pockerley and the museum entrance. **James Millington**

The tramway opened in 1973 and has since been extended several times, firstly into the recreated street, in 1975, and then to the museum entrance in 1988. A final extension, opened in 1993, completed a full circuit, which can be operated both clockwise and anti-clockwise with passing loops provided at Foulbridge, the museum entrance, Pockerley, and the length of double track in the town. The aim is to focus the tram fleet on local exhibits, which has been achieved in part with trams either from or representing the local fleets of Gateshead, Newcastle, South Shields and Sunderland. However, trams from both Blackpool and Sheffield are also resident at the museum and many visitors over the years have added greatly to the variety on offer.

The Route

The tramway is a circular route which is operated in both clockwise and anti-clockwise directions. Clockwise from the passing loop at the museum entrance, the tramway descends a gradient along single track towards the tram depot at Foulbridge, where another passing loop is provided. From here, trams continue on single track again to the recreated town, where double track is provided throughout. A crossover features in the town street, but is rarely used in normal operation. From the town, trams head towards the entrance on a single track alignment to Pockerley, where a further passing loop is provided. The final section of single line between here and the museum entrance is on a steep gradient and is controlled by railway style token block working to ensure safety of operation.

Gateshead 10 has run in its latter day guise as Grimsby & Immingham 26 for a number of years, but is set to return to its original identity during 2016. **James Millington**

Opening Times

The museum is open throughout the year. Opening hours are from 10.00 until 16.00 (October to March) and until 17.00 (March to October). Check website for full details.

Admission Prices

Adult: £18.50   **Senior:** £13.50   **Child:** £10.50
Family *(2 adults and 2 children)*: £48.50
All admission tickets are valid for a full year from the date of issue.

Key Location

The recreated Edwardian street is the focal point of the museum, and provides a superb backdrop against which to admire the trams as they go about their daily business. The tramway features a double track layout through the town street, providing plenty of activity and the opportunity to see trams passing.

No.	Origin	Built	Status
10	Gateshead & District	1925	Undergoing overhaul
16	Sunderland	1900	Operational
31	Blackpool	1901	On loan to Blackpool Transport
49	Newcastle & Gosforth	Unknown	Undergoing restoration *(based on the frame of Leamington & Warwick 8)*
51	Gateshead	1900	Stored
52	Gateshead & District	1901	Stored
114	Newcastle	1901	Operational
196	Oporto	1935	Operational. *Displayed fictitiously in South Shields livery*
147	Blackpool	1924	On loan from Blackpool Transport
264	Sheffield	1907	Overhaul in progress
621	Blackpool	1937	Stored
513	Sheffield	1950	On loan to East Anglia Transport Museum
703	Blackpool *(displayed fictitiously as Sunderland 101)*	1934	Stored
749	Blackpool (tower wagon)	1901	Stored

Fleet details:

East Anglia Transport Museum
Carlton Colville

Vital Statistics

Established: 1972
Operated by: East Anglia Transport Museum Society Limited
Route mileage: approximately 0.25 (0.4km)
Power supply: 550V DC overhead line
Gauge: 4ft 8½in (1435mm)
Address: Chapel Road, Carlton Colville, Lowestoft, NR33 8BL
Website: www.eatransportmuseum.co.uk

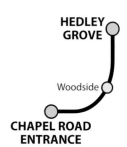

HEDLEY GROVE

Woodside

CHAPEL ROAD ENTRANCE

Background

The East Anglia Transport Museum is located at Carlton Colville, near Lowestoft in Suffolk. Founded in 1965, the museum opened to the public in 1972 and featured a 200 yard long operating tramway along with a trolleybus circuit and a narrow gauge railway. The tramway was doubled in length in 1982 when a 200 yard extension was laid through woodland alongside the Hedley House Hotel, forming the extent of the current line. The extension was originally on land leased from this adjacent business, but in more recent years the land has been acquired by the museum, securing its future.

Sheffield 'Roberts' car 513 arrives back at the Chapel Road terminus as Blackpool 'Standard' 159 prepares to depart.
James Millington

The Route

From the double track stub terminus at Chapel Road, trams run along a recreated street to the left of the three track tram depot, and then passed the front of the adjacent trolleybus depot. At the end of the street running section the track turns sharply left onto a reserved track section through woodland, before terminating at Hedley Grove, where a passing loop is provided.

Opening Times

The museum is open on various dates from April to September, check website for details.

Inside the depot, the restoration of Lowestoft 14 is seen progressing during summer 2015. **James Millington**

Admission Prices

Adult: £9.00   **Senior:** £7.00   **Child:** £6.00

Key Location

Chapel Road terminus is the key location and the only point where trams can be seen side by side. The adjacent trolleybus terminus also adds interest.

Fleet details:			
No.	**Origin**	**Built**	**Status**
11	Blackpool	1939	Operational
14	Lowestoft	1904	Under restoration
159	Blackpool	1927	Operational
474	Amsterdam	1929	Stored
488	Glasgow	1901	Under restoration. Ffestiniog Railway
513	Sheffield	1950	Operational. On loan from Beamish
1858	London	1930	Operational

Black Country Living Museum
Dudley

Vital Statistics

Established: 1979
Operated by: Black Country Living Museum Trust
Route mileage: approximately 0.35 (0.6km)
Power supply: 550V DC overhead line
Gauge: 4ft 8½in (1435mm)
Address: Tipton Road, Dudley, DY1 4SQ
Website: www.bclm.co.uk

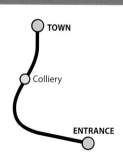

Background

Opened in 1979, the Black Country Museum in Dudley is home to Britain's only 3ft 6in gauge tramway. The line serves transport museum visitors from the museum entrance to the edge of the recreated village, and operates on a reserved track through a typical former Black Country landscape.

Following 34 years operation on basic maintenance, the tramway closed in December 2013 in need of major infrastructure renewal. An 18 month closure followed, but thankfully after the completion of the necessary repairs, it reopened in two stages during July and September 2015.

The Route

From the museum entrance the tramway is a single track route throughout its length. Trams take a right hand curve to a straight section of line that crosses the trolleybus route at a near right angle. The line then bears left alongside the road and terminates close to the recreated town, and alongside the two road tram depot.

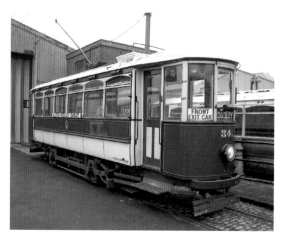

Wolverhampton & District 34 is pictured at the museum entrance about to depart for the recreated town.
James Millington

Opening Times

The museum is open Wednesday to Sunday throughout the year from 10.00 to 16.00 and daily from April to October from 10.00 to 17.00, check website for details.

Wolverhampton Corporation 49 loads passengers at the town terminus alongside the tram depot. **Paul Turner**

Admission Prices

Adult: £16.95 (£15.95 online in advance)
Concessions: £13.50 (£12.50 online in advance)
Child: £8.45 (£7.45 online in advance)
Family *(2 adults and up to 3 children)*: £48.00 (£46.00 online in advance).

Key Location

The crossing with the trolleybus route, adjacent to the entrance to the mine, provides a good location to record photographs of the tramway.

No.	Origin	Built	Status
Fleet details:			
5	Dudley, Stourbridge & District	1920	Under restoration. Llangollen Railway
19	Wolverhampton & District	1902	Stored, awaiting restoration
23	Wolverhampton	1892	Stored, awaiting restoration
34	Wolverhampton & District	1919	Operational
49	Wolverhampton	1909	Operational
75	Dudley, Stourbridge & District	1919	Stored, awaiting restoration
361	Lisbon	1906	Stored

Museum of Scottish Industrial Life
Summerlee

Vital Statistics

Established: 1988
Operated by: North Lanarkshire Council/Summerlee Transport Group
Route mileage: approximately 0.25 (0.4km)
Power supply: 550V DC overhead line
Gauge: 4ft 8½in (1435mm)
Address: Heritage Way, Coatbridge, ML5 1QD
Website: http://www.visitlanarkshire.com/things-to-see-do/museums-and-heritage/summerlee-the-museum-of-scottish-industrial-life/----

Background

The Museum of Scottish Industrial Life opened in March 1988 as the Summerlee Heritage Park. It is based on the site of a former ironworks and benefited from a substantial makeover between 2006-2008 when £10m was invested to improve displays and facilities. The tramway is operated and maintained with support from the Summerlee Transport Group and was the first to re-open in Scotland since the closure of the Glasgow system in 1962.

The Route

Starting from the museum entrance, the tramway takes a gentle right hand curve and crosses Gartsherrie Burn over a stone bridge before arriving at the two road depot. Trams turn sharply right and continue to the terminus adjacent to the miners' cottages. The route is single track throughout.

Opening Times

The museum is open daily, all year round except 25th/26th December and 1st/2nd January, from 10.00 to 17.00 (until 16.00 November – March).

Admission Prices

Admission to the museum is free.
A day ticket for tram rides cost £1.00 and is available from the museum shop.

Key Location

The key location is close to the tram depot, where trams cross the bridge over Gartsherrie Burn.

Fleet details:

No.	Origin	Built	Status
53	Lanarkshire	1908	Operational
392	Dusseldorf	1950	Operational
1017	Glasgow	1904	Operational
1245	Glasgow	1939	Undergoing restoration

Dusseldorf 392 is the museum's access tram and normally provides the winter service on the tramway, as seen here during February 2015. **James Millington**

Wirral Heritage Tramway
Birkenhead

Vital Statistics

Established: 1995
Operated by: Merseyside Tramway Preservation Society
Route mileage: approximately 0.5 (0.8km)
Power supply: 550V DC overhead line
Gauge: 4ft 8½in (1435mm)
Address: 1 Taylor Street, Birkenhead, CH41 1BG
Website: www.mtps.co.uk

**TAYLOR STREET
DEPOT & MUSEUM**

Pacific Road

**WOODSIDE
FERRY**

Background

In 1860 George Francis Train introduced the tram to Britain when he founded his first horse drawn tramway in Birkenhead. In recognition of this remarkable feat, which saw Birkenhead become the birthplace of the tram in the UK, and as part of a project to rehabilitate for tourism former dock land along the banks of the River Mersey, Wirral Borough Council began planning during 1987 for a tramway museum and a short heritage tramway which was opened in stages from April 1995. Two heritage pattern trams were constructed in Hong Kong for the inauguration of the line. In partnership with the Merseyside Tramway Preservation Society, these were supplemented by a fleet of magnificently restored trams, most of local origin, over the succeeding years.

Liverpool 'Baby Grand' 245 returned to use in 2015 following a lengthy restoration having not run since the closure of the Liverpool system in 1957. **James Millington**

The line is the only 'museum' tramway in the UK which runs in public streets, and its operation was originally in the hands of Blackpool Transport Services Ltd which undertook the testing and commissioning of the new trams and trained the crews. Wirral Council took control in 2006 but thereafter followed a number of years of uncertainty when, due to local government spending cuts, the Council attempted to divest itself of responsibility towards the tramway and to dispose of buildings associated with it, including the depot and museum at Taylor Street. The situation was finally resolved during early 2014 when responsibility for the tramway operation was handed directly to the Merseyside Tramway Preservation Society, under whose guidance it will hopefully enjoy a secure future.

The Route

The museum and two road depot are located at Taylor Street, at the far end of the tramway. Trams load opposite the depot then depart on a single track tramway, turning right along a short reservation leading to a right angle crossing with Canning Street, which is protected by traffic signals. The route continues around a reverse curve and a sharp right turn past Egerton Bridge, to run along a straight section at the side of the Wirral Metropolitan College. Trams then run alongside Shore Road to Pacific Road, where there is a passing loop (unusually operated with right hand running), and past the site of the former depot, which is still connected to the line. Trams continue to follow Shore Road and then briefly join it before a sharp left curve takes them down to the Woodside Ferry terminus, which features a double track terminal stub.

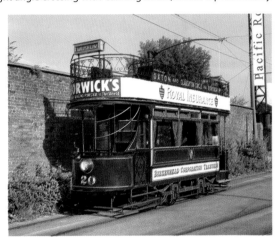

Birkenhead 20 waits in the passing loop at Pacific Road, the halfway point of the line. **James Millington**

Opening Times

The tramway operates on Saturdays and Sundays between 13.00 and 17.00, and on Bank Holidays and during school holidays (Wednesday to Friday) between 13.00 and 16.30. Check website for details.

Fares

Payable to conductor

Adult: return tram ride £2.00   **Concession and child:** return tram ride £1.00.

Key Location

Woodside Ferry terminus is the focal point of the heritage tramway, and is situated adjacent to the boarding stage for the Mersey Ferries service and the 'U-boat Story', which includes a sectioned genuine German U-boat. The Liverpool skyline, featuring the 'Three Graces' of the Royal Liver Building, the Port of Liverpool Building and the Cunard Building can be seen across the river. It was in front of these, at Pier Head, that many of Liverpool's original tram services once terminated.

On display inside the depot and museum at Taylor Street is Liverpool double deck horse car 43. **James Millington**

Fleet details:

No.	Origin	Built	Status
20	Birkenhead	1900	Operational
28	Warrington	1902	Undergoing restoration*
43	Liverpool	1890	Stored (Pacific Road)
69	Birkenhead (Hong Kong)	1992	Operational
70	Birkenhead (Hong Kong)	1992	Operational
78	Wallasey	1920	Operational
245	Liverpool	1938	Operational
730	Lisbon	1930	Operational
762	Liverpool	1931	Operational

Collections

National Transport Museum
Howth, Ireland

Vital Statistics

Established: 1971
Operated by: Transport Museum Society of Ireland
Address: Heritage Depot, Howth Demesne, Howth, Dublin 13
Telephone: 01 832 0427
Email: info@nationaltransportmuseum.org
Website: www.nationaltransportmuseum.org

Background

Located at Howth Demesne, Howth, approximately eight miles north east of Dublin, the volunteer run National Transport Museum of Ireland is the custodian of a number of tramcars of Irish heritage. Included in the collection is an ex-London trailer restored to represent a former Dublin trailer in its latter day electrified condition.

Opening Times

The museum is open on Saturdays, Sundays and Bank Holidays from 14.00 until 17.00, check website for details.

Admission Prices

Adult: €3.00   **Senior:** €1.25   **Child:** €1.25   **Family:** €8.00

Fleet details:

No.	Origin	Built	Status
N/a	Dublin United (Director's car)	1901	Static display
9	Giant's Causeway	1889	Static display
9	Hill of Howth	1902	Static display
253	Dublin United	1928	Static display
284	Dublin United	1928	Static display
T124	London County Council (trailer)	1915	Static display – fictitiously as Dublin 224

Streetlife Museum of Transport
Hull

Vital Statistics

Established: 1989
Operated by: Hull Museums
Address: Museums Quarter, High Street, Hull, HU1 1PS
Telephone: 01482 613902
Email: info@hullcc.gov.uk
Website: www.hullcc.gov.uk

Background

The current museum opened in 1989 and has a range of galleries showcasing the exhibits in settings relating to their past. The three trams are displayed in a recreated period street scene and include Ryde Pier car 3, dating from 1871, which is reputed to be the oldest surviving tramcar in Britain.

Opening Times

The museum is open daily from 10.00 until 17.00 (from 13.30 until 16.30 on Sundays), check website for details.

Hull 132, as viewed from a mezzanine gallery at the Hull Streetlife Museum.
James Millington

Admission Prices

Admission to the Streetlife Museum of Transport is free.

Fleet details:			
No.	**Origin**	**Built**	**Status**
1	Portstewart	1882	Static display
3	Ryde Pier	1871	Static display
132	Hull	1909	Static display. On loan from TMS, Crich

Riverside Museum
Glasgow

Vital Statistics

Established: 2011
Operated by: Glasgow Life
Address: Riverside Museum, 100 Pointhouse Place, Glasgow, G3 8RS
Telephone: 0141 287 2720
Email: museums@glasgowlife.org.uk
Website: www.glasgowlife.org.uk/museums/riverside

Background

The Riverside Museum, located on the bank of the River Clyde in Glasgow, is the new home of the collection of the Glasgow Transport Museum, previously housed at Kelvin Hall. The collection was established in 1962 following the closure of Glasgow's tramway system and was originally located in the former tram workshops at Coplawhill depot in Pollokshields. The tram collection spans the history of operations in the city and includes examples of the first horse and electric trams right through to the very last tram built for, and indeed by, Glasgow Corporation, in 1952.

Glasgow Cunarder 1392 is one of the centrepiece exhibits at the Riverside Museum. Built as recently as 1952, it spent only a short time in service in Glasgow. The surrounding exhibits make it hard to photograph.
Tony Caddick

Opening Times

The museum is open daily from 10.00 until 17.00 (from 11.00 Friday and Sunday), check website for details.

Admission Prices

Admission to Riverside Museum is free.

Fleet details:			
No.	**Origin**	**Built**	**Status**
543	Horse car	1894	Static display
672	Room and Kitchen single deck car	1898	Static display
779	Unvestibuled, balcony Standard	1900	Static display
1088	Enclosed Standard	1924	Static display
1089	Experimental single deck car	1926	Static display
1173	Coronation	1938	Static display
1392	Cunarder	1952	Static display

London Transport Museum

Vital Statistics

Established: 1980
Operated by: Transport for London
Addresses: London Transport Museum, Covent Garden Piazza, London, WC2E 7BB
Acton Museum Depot, 118-120 Gunnersbury Lane, Acton Town, London, W3 9BQ
Telephone: 020 7565 6344
Email: bookings@ltmuseum.co.uk
Website: www.ltmuseum.co.uk

Background

The London Transport Museum exists to conserve the transport history of London and has been based in Covent Garden since 1980, following a move from the previous facility at Syon Park. It was extensively refurbished between 2005 and 2007, with some exhibits moving to Acton Museum Depot.

Opening Times

The museum at Covent Garden is open daily throughout the year from 10.00 (11.00 on Fridays) until 18.00. Acton Museum Depot is opened two to three times a year, check website for details.

Admission Prices

Adult: £16.00   **Senior:** £13.50   **Child** *(under 17)*: Free
Tickets allow unlimited entry for 12 months.

Fleet details:			
No.	**Origin**	**Built**	**Status**
102	West Ham	1910	Static display – Covent Garden
284	London Tramways Co.	1881	Static display – Covent Garden
355	Metropolitan Electric Tramways	1931	Static display – Acton depot
1025	London Transport (ex-L.C.C.)	1908	Static display – Acton depot

Jurby Transport Museum
Isle of Man

Vital Statistics

Established: 2010
Operated by: Manx Transport Trust Limited
Address: Hangar 230, Jurby Industrial Estate, Jurby, Isle of Man, IM7 3BD
Email: jtminfo@manx.net
Website: www.jtmiom.im

Background

The museum is situated in a former aircraft hangar, now part of Jurby Industrial Estate, and features a wide ranging display of transport exhibits which demonstrate the rich history of the Isle of Man.

Opening Times

The museum is open on Tuesdays, Saturdays, Sundays and Bank Holidays from 10.00 until 16.00 from April to September, and on Sundays from 10.00 until 18.00 from October to April, check website for details.

Admission Prices

Admission to Jurby Transport Museum is free.

Fleet details:			
No.	**Origin**	**Built**	**Status**
11	Douglas Bay Horse Tramway	1886	Static display
22	Douglas Bay Horse Tramway	1890	Static display and shop
47	Douglas Bay Horse Tramway	1911	Static display
72/73	Douglas Upper Cable Tramway	1896	Static display
N/a	Ramsey Pier (locomotive and coach)	1937	Static display

NEETT, Sunderland
(North Eastern Electrical Transport Trust)

Vital Statistics

Established: 2012
Operated by: NEETT, in partnership with the North East Land, Sea and Air Museums Trust
Address: Old Washington Road, Sunderland, Tyne & Wear, SR5 3HZ
Email: info@neett.co.uk
Website: www.neett.co.uk/www.nelsam.org.uk

Background

The North Eastern Electrical Traction Trust is based at the premises of the North East Land, Sea and Air Museum near Sunderland. Essentially interested in all forms of electric traction, the group purchased a number of redundant trams from Blackpool in 2011 and have also taken under their wings two foreign trams that had been in the UK for many years but which previously had no secure future. The most recent addition is the former Blackpool illuminated 'Hovertram' 735 which had previously been at the Beith Transport Museum in Scotland. Following the construction of a brand new depot during 2013/14, most of the collection is housed undercover.

Opening Times

The North East Land, Sea and Air Museums site is open daily from 10.00 until 17.00 from April to October, and from 10.00 until dusk from November to March, check website for details.

Admission Prices

Adult: £5.00   **Senior:** £3.00   **Child:** £3.00
Family *(2 adults and 2 children)*: £13.00

Fleet details:

No.	Origin	Built	Status
210	Graz	1949	In store
412	Krefeld	1957	Static display
647	Blackpool	1988	Static display
674	Blackpool	1961*	Static display
684	Blackpool	1960	Static display
708	Blackpool	1934	Static display. On loan from MTMS, Manchester
721	Blackpool	1935	Under restoration
735	Blackpool	1963	Static display

* Indicates date rebuilt from an earlier car

Ulster Folk & Transport Museum
Cultra

Vital Statistics
Established: 1967
Operated by: National Museums Northern Ireland
Address: 153 Bangor Road, Holywood, BT18 0EU
Telephone: 028 9042 8428
Website: www.uftm.org.uk

Background
The Ulster Folk and Transport Museum is located on the main A2 road at Cultra, approximately seven miles east of Belfast. The museum consists of two sites, either side of the main road, with the transport collection housed in two halls on one side. In one is displayed the Irish Railway Collection, which includes the Portstewart steam tram engine, whilst the trams are housed in the other building alongside an impressive selection of historic road vehicles.

Opening Times
The museum is open Tuesday to Sunday from 10.00 until 16.00 (from 11.00 at weekends) from October to February, and from 10.00 until 17.00 from March to September, check website for details.

Admission Prices
Adult: £9.00   **Senior:** £7.00
Child: £5.50   **Family** (2 adults and 3 children): £25.00

Please note admission to the Folk and Transport Museums are charged separately, although a combined adult 'same day' ticket can be purchased for a slight premium.

Fleet details:			
No.	**Origin**	**Built**	**Status**
2	Bessbrook & Newry	1885	Static display
2	Giant's Causeway (trailer)	1883	Static display
2	Portstewart (steam tram loco)	1900	Static display
4	Hill of Howth	1901	Static display
5	Giant's Causeway (trailer)	1883	Static display
118	Belfast (horse car)	1885	Static display
249	Belfast	1905	Static display
357	Belfast	1929	Static display
381	Fintona (horse car)	1883	Static display

Aberystwyth Cliff Railway

Vital Statistics

Opened: 1896
Gauge: 4ft 8.5in
Route Length: 778 feet
Lift Height: 430 feet
Gradient: 1 in 2
Journey Time: 2 minutes 20 seconds
Address: Cliff Railway House, Cliff Terrace, Aberystwyth, Ceredigion, SY23 2DN
Telephone: 01970 617642
Operated by: Constitution Hill Ltd
Website: www.aberystwythcliffrailway.co.uk

Due to the steep 1 in 2 incline, the cars are stepped as can be seen here, along with open balconies at each end. The period advertising for Brasso Metal Polish is a nice touch. 3rd August 2013. **Alan Crawshaw**

This funicular was built to transport customers to the site of an early Victorian theme park, which consisted of arcades, with a restaurant at the bottom and a Camera Obscura and park at the top. Designed by George Croydon Marks, it was operated on a water balance system until it was upgraded to electric power in 1921. At 778 feet the line is the longest electrically operated British funicular railway. An unusual feature is that the deep cutting it runs through. The line is now run by the charity Constitution Hill Ltd, a group of local volunteers.

Babbacombe Cliff Railway

Vital Statistics

Opened: 1926
Gauge: 5ft
Route Length: 720 feet
Lift Height: 256 feet
Gradient: 1 in 2.88
Journey Time: 2 minutes 25 seconds
Address: Babbacombe Downs Road, Torquay, TQ1 3LF
Telephone: 01803 328750
Operated by: Babbacombe Cliff Railway Community Interest Company
Website: www.babbacombecliffrailway.co.uk

One of the last traditionally built cliff lifts in the country, Babbacombe Cliff Railway was the work of the Torquay Tramway Company, set up in 1923 with the intention of installing a lift to Oddicombe Beach (to link Torquay). Work at a cost of £15,648 started in December 1924 and the lift opened in 1926, to transport passengers from the cliff tops to the beach. Designed by George Croydon Marks, who by this time had considerable experience of this work, it was built by Waygood Otis. The line only worked for nine years before it was bought by Torquay Corporation for £18,000 in 1935. In 1941 the beach was sealed off for security due to the Second World War and the lift closed until 1951, when £10,000 was spent on refurbishment after ten years of disuse. 2003 saw it closed for six weeks after the safety gear stopped the lift half way and the passengers had to be rescued. The railway is once again open for business and in 2009 ownership transferred to the Babbacombe Cliff Railway Community Interest Company. The cars are large for a cliff lift with a capacity of 40 passengers and are designed to have the appearance of a traditional tramcar. An interesting feature of the line is the ringing of a bell at the bottom station to advise any passengers that the lift will close in 30 and 15 minutes. This bell was rescued from a Scandinavian vessel, Talga. If you are inclined, you can have a wedding service on board one of the 'trams'!

One of the passenger cars is seen at the top station, with the pulley to the bottom left. The crest is a nice touch.
expat a

East Cliff Railway
Bournemouth

Vital Statistics

Opened: 1908
Gauge: 5ft 8in
Route Length: 166 feet
Lift Height: 118 feet
Gradient: 1 in 1.5
Journey Time: 55 seconds
Address: East Overcliff Drive, Meyrick Road, Bournemouth
Telephone: 01202 451781
Operated by: Bournemouth Borough Council
Website: www.bournemouth.co.uk/attraction/east-cliff-lift/

Bournemouth East Cliff Lift is the oldest of 3 operating lifts in Bournemouth and opened on 16th April 1908. It was built by Waygood - Otis and Harrison & Co., and links an art gallery and museum on the East Cliff with the beach. The cars are very similar in style to those on the Fisherman's Walk Lift; they were built as recently as 2007 and carry 12 passengers. The previous cars were built in the 1960s and had an aluminium shell. The lift was electrically operated with a 25hp motor from its inception. Originally a driver was based at the top station with an assistant at the bottom station. This continued until 1987 when an electronic control system was installed.

The 2007 built cars are seen about to arrive at their respective stations on 26th June 2013. They carry a rather plain and simple livery on this short but steep line. **Elliot Brown**

West Cliff Railway
Bournemouth

Vital Statistics

Opened: 1908
Gauge: 5ft 8in
Route Length: 102 feet
Lift Height: 118 feet
Gradient: 1 in 1.42
Journey Time: 40 seconds
Address: St Michaels Road, West Cliff, Bournemouth
Telephone: 01202 451781
Operated by: Bournemouth Borough Council
Website: www.bournemouth.co.uk/attraction/west-cliff-lift/

The cars are all very similar in Bournemouth, although the West Cliff Lift has a slightly more varied livery, with the application of a coat of dark brown paint. 3rd July 2015. **Andrew Murray**

Like the East Cliff Lift, the West Cliff Lift was also built by Waygood-Otis and Harrison & Co. It also opened in 1908, although slightly later on 1st August 1908. Similar to all of Bournemouth's cliff lifts, the original cars were based on the town's tram cars, these were originally powered by a 25 hp electric motor, operated by a driver at the top and an assistant at the bottom. This was replaced in the 1960s by a 28 hp three phase motor. Also in the 1960s new aluminium bodied cars were built, designed to be interchangeable between all three of the town's cliff lifts. 1987 saw the full length of the track replaced and the 1990s saw the installation of an electronic control system.

Fisherman's Walk Cliff Lift
Bournemouth

Vital Statistics

Opened: 1935
Gauge: 5ft 10in
Route Length: 128 feet
Lift Height: 91 feet
Gradient: 1 in 1.5
Journey Time: 50 seconds
Address: Southbourne Overcliff Drive, Bournemouth
Telephone: 01202 451781
Operated by: Bournemouth Borough Council
Website: http://bournemouth.co.uk/attraction/fishermans-walk-lift/

Built in 1935 by Bournemouth Corporation and designed by the borough engineer Mr F P Delamore, the UK's shortest cliff lift is just 128 feet long. It was designed to serve the Southbourne and Boscombe promenades and has two 12 seater passenger cars. The lift was originally powered by a 21 hp 500V DC motor which was replaced in the 1960s. It is a very simple little line, with modest stations at both ends.

The proximity of the two stations is easily understood from this photo taken on16th June 2015, although it saves a walk up a steep cliff! **Alwyn Ladell**

Bridgnorth Cliff Railway

Vital Statistics

Opened: 1892
Gauge: 3ft 8.5in
Route Length: 201 feet
Lift Height: 111 feet
Gradient: 1 in 1.81
Journey Time: 1 minute 25 seconds
Address: 6a Castle Terrace, Bridgnorth, WV16 4AH
Telephone: 01746 762052
Operated by: Bridgnorth Castle Hill Railway Company Ltd
Website: www.bridgnorthcliffrailway.co.uk

The unique style and liveries used on the Bridgnorth Castle Hill Railway cars are clearly seen in this view taken on 24th October 2015. **Simon Ingham**

This line was opened on 7th July 1892 by George Croydon Marks, who unusually became the first Managing Director, closely followed by his brother Edward. The line links the Low Town of Bridgnorth with the High Town, opposite Bridgnorth Castle, and is England's only inland electric cliff railway. When first opened, it was powered by a system using water and gravity: water was pumped into a 2,000 gallon tank beneath the top car until its weight overcame the lower car. The tank was emptied once the car reached the lower station. Unusually the cliff lift was rebuilt during the war years of 1943 and 1944 and modified to use electricity, reopening on 9th May 1944. The original cars were replaced in 1955 by the distinctive aluminium monocoque ones still used today. Also in 1955 a new winding gear was installed below the top station, of the same type as formerly used in collieries. The railway is still run by the original owning company and in 2011 was in the hands of the cousins of the founder George Croydon Marks.

Leas Cliff Lift
Folkestone

Vital Statistics

Opened: 1885
Gauge: 5ft 10in
Route Length: 164 feet
Lift Height: 100 feet
Gradient: 1 in 1.192
Journey Time: 50 seconds
Address: Lower Sandgate Road, Folkestone, CT20 1QJ
Telephone: 01303 210047
Operated by: Leas Lift Community Interest Company
Website: www.grand-uk.com/leaslift.html

This is one of the oldest water-balance cliff lifts still in operation, and opened on 16th September 1885. It is of the water and gravity system, operated from a small cabin at the top of the cliff, and all the water is recycled. Due to its phenomenal success, a second was installed alongside in 1888; although now disused, those tracks can still be seen and two more were built further along the Leas cliff, showing the area's popularity. Formerly in private ownership, the lift was taken over in 1967 by the local council. In 2009 when the lease expired, it passed into the hands of The Leas Lift Community Interest Company, following the council's decision that the lift was too expensive to maintain. Two years later in 2011, significant restoration work was undertaken which included mechanical work, re-profiling the cars' tyres, replacement of steel work in the water storage tanks, replacing the electrical wiring and overhauls of the power pumps.

The beautifully kept lift at Folkestone is seen with several vintage cars at the bottom station, the disused lift is on the right. 19th September 2010. **Terry Blackman**

West Hill Railway
Hastings

Vital Statistics

Opened: 1891
Gauge: 6ft
Route Length: 500 feet
Lift Height: 170 feet
Gradient: 1 in 2.9
Journey Time: 1 minute 40 seconds
Address: West Hill, George Street, Hastings
Telephone: 01424 451111
Operated by: Hastings Borough Council
Website: www.visit1066country.com/things-to-do/attractions/cliff-railways-p411571

Hastings West Hill Railway has the very unusual feature of a tunnel! By its very nature this is exceptionally rare for a cliff lift. The exquisitely built brickwork of the tunnel and sides can be seen to good effect. **Kevin Geraghty-Shewan**

The Hastings West Hill Railway, or West Hill Lift, as it is more commonly referred to, opened on 7th July 1892, powered by a gas engine. An unusual feature is that it runs predominantly within a tunnel for 402 feet of its 500 feet length! It offers a useful link between George Street in the Old Town to Hastings Castle and St. Clement's Caves and has great views of Beachy Head. The line's first operator, The Hastings Lift Company, built the lift despite local opposition. Construction costs doubled, putting the line into financial difficulty. Following bankruptcy in 1894, the line was taken over by The Hastings Passenger Lift Company which ran it until 1947 when it was bought by the local council. 1971 saw the line converted to electric operation. To celebrate its centenary year in 1991 a full refurbishment was carried out.

East Hill Railway
Hastings

Vital Statistics

Opened: 1903
Gauge: 5ft
Route Length: 267 feet
Lift Height: 261 feet
Gradient: 1 in 1.28
Journey Time: 54 seconds
Address: Rock-a-Nore Road, Hastings
Telephone: 01424 451111
Operated by: Hastings Borough Council
Website: www.visit1066country.com/things-to-do/attractions/cliff-railways-p411571

Opened in 1903 by Hastings Borough Council, this is the steepest funicular railway in Great Britain with a gradient of 1 in 2.8. It provides access to Hastings Country Park overlooking Rock-a-Nore, with the lower part of the line running in a rock cutting. Originally worked on the water-based principle, for which the twin towers at the top station were used as water tanks, the line was converted to run on electricity in 1973-76 and new cars replaced the original ones. Unfortunately the line closed in 2007 after a control panel fault didn't stop the cars correctly so both were damaged. A huge investment began in 2008 with new cars, new control gear and associated safety systems as well as repairs to the damaged station, allowing re-opening in March 2010.

The Hastings East Hill Railway has very attractive top and bottom stations. The ACDC poster adds to the electric theme!
Terry Blackman

Lynton & Lynmouth Cliff Railway

Vital Statistics

Opened: 1890
Gauge: 3ft 9in
Route Length: 862 feet
Lift Height: 500 feet
Gradient: 1 in 1.75
Journey Time: 2 minutes 30 seconds
Address: Lee Road, Lynton, EX35 6HW
Telephone: 01598 735908
Operated by: Lynmouth & Lynton Lift Co
Website: www.cliffrailwaylynton.co.uk

Opened on Easter Monday in 1890 between the twin towns of Lynton and Lynmouth as a water powered funicular railway, is another example designed by George Croydon Marks. Unusually it has an intermediate stop below Lynton Station, which was used to transport goods. The car body could be removed to transport bulky items, including cars! The two operating cars, each with room for 40 passengers, are joined by a continuous cable running around a pulley at each end of the incline. Water is fed through a pipe from the West Lyn River and fills tanks fixed underneath the car at the top of the incline. Water is released from the lower car until the top car descends, with speed controlled by a brakeman inside each car. In recognition of its historic nature the railway is classified as a listed monument.

The steep gradient and length of the railway can be glimpsed in this photo as well as the open balconies, making this a very popular tourist attraction. 18th July 2015. **Mark Hows**

Saltburn Cliff Lift

Vital Statistics

Opened: 1884
Gauge: 4ft 2in
Route Length: 207 feet
Lift Height: 120 feet
Gradient: 1 in 1.40
Journey Time: 55 seconds
Address: Lower Promenade, Saltburn, TS12 2QX
Telephone: 01287 622528
Operated by: Redcar and Cleveland Borough Council
Website: www.saltburnbysea.com/html/clifflift.html

Replacing a mechanical hoist which had been declared unsafe the previous year, this lift was designed and installed by George Croydon Marks, opening on 28th June 1884. It is operated by water, which flows into tanks underneath the car at the top station, so the weight takes it down the gradient and also pulls the other car up. Once it reaches the bottom the tank is emptied. It was originally powered by a four-cylinder Crossley combustion engine pump, which survived until 1913 when a DC generator and pump were installed. This

Looking down the steep gradient the bottom station can be glimpsed. The facilities here are among the most lavish in the UK for a cliff lift.
James Millington

in turn was replaced relatively quickly when in 1924 an AC electrically operated water pump was installed, which is still in use. The operation is controlled by a brakeman who sits in a small cabin at the top. The bottom however has very lavish buildings which include a ticket office, waiting room and engine room, sharing a similarity with all cliff lifts, in that the traffic is always busier going up hill! Following the Second World War the lift was bought by the council. Originally the cars had stained glass windows but these were lost when the car bodies were replaced in 1955. They were again replaced in 1979 (based on the original design) and stained glass windows were installed in 1991. The braking wheel was replaced for the first time in 1998. 2014 saw a full refurbishment of the top station, to original design. The Saltburn Cliff Lift is the oldest water balanced funicular in the United Kingdom.

The carriages were restored in 2010 and returned in Easter 2011, just in time for the town's 150th anniversary.

Scarborough Spa Cliff Lift

Vital Statistics

Opened: 1875
Gauge: 4ft 8.5in
Route Length: 286 feet
Lift Height: 84 feet
Gradient: 1 in 1.75
Journey Time: 47 seconds
Address: Scarborough Spa, South Bay, Scarborough, YO11 2HD
Telephone: 01273 376774
Operated by: Scarborough Spa
Website: www.scarboroughspa.co.uk/cliff_lift

Opened by the Scarborough South Cliff Tramway Company Limited on 6th July 1875, this was the first funicular railway in the United Kingdom, built to link the South Cliff Esplanade to the Scarborough Spa. The line was built by Crossley Brothers of Manchester and the carriages were built by the Metropolitan Carriage Company of Birmingham. Initially the cars were moved by a counterweight system, with water tanks carried under each car, the water being pumped using a hydraulic system powered by gas engines. These only lasted four years and were replaced in 1879 by steam pumps, which continued in service until a major refurbishment in 1934-35 by Hudswell, Clarke & Company, traditionally a steam engine builder. (Incidentally this company also built two diesel powered steam outline locomotives for the nearby North Bay Railway in 1931 and 1932). A new electric motor was installed and the cars were replaced, surviving to this day with little change except slight modifications providing better access for passengers. Scarborough Borough Council purchased the lift in 1993 and made the operation completely automatic in 1997.

One of the 1934-5 cars is seen at the bottom Spa station in March 2014. Many of the car's original features can be seen. **David Umpleby**

Central Tramway
Scarborough

Vital Statistics

Opened: 1881
Gauge: 4ft 8.5in
Route Length: 234 feet
Lift Height: 81 feet
Gradient: 1 in 2.8
Journey Time: 38 seconds
Address: Marine Parade, Scarborough, YO11 2ER
Telephone: 01723 501754
Operated by: Central Tramway Company
Website: www.centraltramwaysscarborough.blogspot.co.uk

The Central Tramway Company was formed in 1880 and began operations on 1st August 1881, making it the oldest tramway company still in existence. The line runs between the town centre (north side of The Grand Hotel) and the beach. Originally powered by steam, the steam house was situated away from the tramway at the top station. Drivers had no view of the cars and had to rely on markings on a rope to stop the cars in the correct unloading place. 1910 saw the power supply changed to electricity and in 1932 the motor was placed under the top station, meaning the cars could now be driven from the top station. The cars were also replaced in the same year. In 1975 a fire damaged the carriages, with replacements purchased from George Neville Truck Equipment of Kirby in Ashfield. In 2009 an automated drive system was installed along with new motors. Three years later in 2012 significant restoration of the buildings and carriages took place, making this a superb example of a working cliff lift.

An ascending car will shortly stop at the top station on a quiet March day in 2014, with the traditionally painted cars adding to the historic feel. **David Umpleby**

Southend Cliff Lift

Vital Statistics

Opened: 1912
Gauge: 4ft 6in
Route Length: 130 feet
Lift Height: 57 feet
Gradient: 1 in 2.28
Journey Time: 1 minute 30 seconds
Address: Royal Terrace, Southend on Sea
Telephone: 01702 212345
Operated by: Southend Museums Service
Website: www.southendmuseums.co.uk/page/Historic-Cliff-Lift

The unusual Southend Cliff lift only has one track and one carriage and therefore limited capacity. The large passenger car has a lot of similarities to a garden shed! **Janet Penn**

Southend council installed one of the country's first moving walkways in 1901, a radical approach, which was an experimental fore-runner of the escalator. This was replaced by a new tramway, built by Waygood and Co. and opened in 1912. The Southend Cliff Railway is very unusual because it only has one carriage! This is balanced by a counterweight running underneath the main track. 1930 saw improvements and a new carriage, then 1959 saw new upper and lower stations and another new carriage. A third carriage replaced the 1959 built one in 1990 which had the benefits of improved access for pushchairs and the disabled. In 2003 a malfunction forced it out of action, after which it lay idle for seven years. An official re-opening by the Mayor of Southend took place on 25th May 2010.

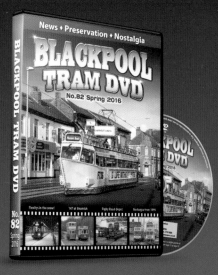